CW00747493

UNSECURED LENDING RISK MANAGEMENT

UNSECURED LENDING RISK MANAGEMENT

A PRACTITIONER'S GUIDE

FRANK TIAN

Copyright © 2021 by Gangxing Frank Tian

All rights reserved. No part of this publication may be reproduced, distributed, or transmitted in any form or by any means, including photocopying, recordings, or other electronic or mechanical methods, without the prior written permission of the publisher.

Green Wheat Publishing, Oshawa, Ontario, Canada. Tel: (416)-951-3990.

Quantity sales: special discounts are available on quantity purchases by corporations, associations, educational institutions, and others. For details, please contact the publisher.

Limit of Liability/Disclaimer of Warranty: This book is for general information use only. While the publisher and author have used their best efforts in preparing the book, they make no representations or warranties with respect to the accuracy or completeness of the contents of this book and specifically disclaim any implied warranties of merchantability or fitness for a particular purpose. The advice and strategies contained herein may not be suitable for your situation. Neither the publisher nor author shall be liable for any loss that may result from the reliance by any person or entity on the information in this book.

Unsecured Lending Risk Management – A Practitioner's Guide
First Edition
By Gangxing Frank Tian

ISBN: 978-1-7775927-0-7 (paperback)
      978-1-7775927-2-1 (hardcover)
      978-1-7775927-1-4 (ebook)

Cover photograph © Jinzhu Tian.

Photograph of Frank Tian © Gangxing Frank Tian.

TO MY GRANDMOTHER
(GREAT-AUNT)

Table of Contents

SECTION IV
RISK INFRASTRUCTURE 179

SECTION V
PORTFOLIO RISK MANAGEMENT 217

Acknowledgments

I have had the thoughts for this book for a while. The COVID-19 pandemic made me work from home, like many others, since March 2020. This saved me quite a lot of time that was previously being spent on commuting or driving my kid to the hockey arena and different after-school programs.

Thus, I decided to put the additional time to good use.

Plagues and pandemics have shaped human history; they are also parts of my family story. My paternal grandfather and grandmother contracted hepatitis and pulmonary tuberculosis respectively in their 30s — both of which were fatal diseases in China in the 1940s. When they passed away a week apart from each other, my father was only 4 and his sister was 5. My grandfather's younger brother and his wife raised the two orphans and cared for the great-grandmother, even though, as farmers, they did not possess great means.

When my sister and I were born, we also spent the first few years of our childhood with my great-aunt and great-uncle while my parents were busy working. To us, they are our grandmother and grandfather. My grandfather (great-uncle) passed away 10 years ago and my grandmother (great-aunt) is currently 91. Besides her late brother's two children, she also raised seven of her own. Today, the large family has its members working in diverse occupations in multiple countries. During the reunion held during festivals, it is even difficult to fit everyone in grandmother's two-bedroom apartment.

My family is an example of how human beings struggle against a pandemic together, with love and perseverance. I thus dedicate this book to my grandmother and wish her great health and happiness always.

The knowledge presented in this book has been accumulated over time, as I have had the opportunity to work at several financial institutions in the U.S. and Canada. I thank all my colleagues in risk and other functions within these institutions, the business partners from various service providers, and the thought leaders at industry conferences and seminars. Risk management is not something you perform in isolation. It is a truly collaborative action.

My special thanks go to Mr. Bryan Leaver, whose thorough feedback made the content of this book more complete. I also appreciate the help and encouragement from Ling Qin, Niranjan Kulkarni, and many other friends who reviewed the manuscript.

I thank my parents, who offered me excellent educational opportunities and always provide unconditional support. I thank my sister Yuqian and her husband Changchun, who were always ready to extend a helping hand over the years.

Last but not least, I thank my wife Lucy and my son Max, who truly offered the biggest incentives for me to write and complete this book.

Frank
February 2021

SECTION I
INTRODUCTION

Chapter 1

Introduction

Since starting my career in unsecured lending risk management, I've had many opportunities to share the world of retail risk management with those who have curious minds. That was often over a coffee, prior to the pandemic.

As we are still battling steadfastly with the once-a-century pandemic in the winter of 2021, the need for informational interviews continues. Many in-person communications simply become virtual ones.

As I realized that some questions appear repeatedly, even at the workplace, the idea of a book began to emerge. Even with the current explosion of information, a book is still a good way to organize the information around a subject more systematically and go into a certain amount of depth. This is also a way for me to transfer my knowledge back to the risk community.

In this chapter, I start with who will benefit from this book. I then talk about the approaches I've taken to write the book and, finally, provide a brief overview of how this book is structured.

1.1   Who this book is for

This book is for anyone who would like to understand the practice of unsecured consumer lending risk management and is willing to achieve that by dedicating some time to reading on the subject.

There are several groups of people I kept in mind when writing this book.

People in the Early Stage of Risk Management Career

First, this book is for people who are at an early stage of their risk management career. You might already have one to five years of experience under your belt. With the typical way that risk roles are designed, you have probably worked in a couple of decision areas within the full credit life cycle.

This book is meant to accelerate your learning of retail risk management in general and help establish an overview. Once the framework of concepts is established, it will help you understand how a particular project you are taking on fits into the organization's overall strategic plan.

This book can also serve as a quick training session. Your employer might be able to send you to some corporate training hosted by service providers, but such training opportunity usually just comes by once a year. For some, their company doesn't have the budget to provide such learning opportunities.

You should definitely embrace the corporate training provided by your employer — it is beneficial for you, and a corporate training course often costs thousands of dollars. However, the training modules usually focus on particular tools or specific areas that the service provider specializes in. This book is meant to be supplementary to those trainings.

The other way to acquire knowledge is via on-the-job learning, sometimes mentored by your manager. However, when the organization's structure becomes flatter, the previous training and mentoring responsibility delegated to managers begins to get lost in some institutions. Junior staff members need to take the responsibility for career development into their own hands. This book can serve as a tool for you to check what things you have learned and which body of knowledge you should plan to acquire in order to become a well-rounded risk professional.

Professionals in Other Functions at a Lender

If you are not currently working in the risk function and don't plan to, but are working in other functions within the consumer lending business, such as marketing, product, audit, customer service, collection operations, and credit system, or as service providers, there is still value to be gained in understanding how your risk peers operate on a daily basis.

This is because many of the risk initiatives involve business partners from diverse functions, and thus truly require the collaboration of a cross-functional team.

Understanding how risk decisions typically get made and how they could impact the retail portfolio as levers could 1) make your collaboration with risk on key initiatives easier, and 2) help you plan your own initiatives that could leverage risk's strength.

Once you have a good understanding of risk management practices, your conversations with your risk colleagues will become more productive. If nothing else, it could save hours that otherwise would be spent on the explanation of some standard terminology and concepts.

Plus, it certainly would add weight to your voice during a conversation if you show some level of understanding of how risk management works.

People who are Exploring a Career in Retail Risk Management

There are also those who want to explore the area of retail risk management and see if they could have a career in this field. If that is the case, then this book is definitely for you.

Over the years, I have talked to many people who wanted to explore the world of risk management. Many were students who were about to graduate or had just graduated from their undergraduate or graduate programs. They had heard about the profession of risk management and wanted to explore this line of work. Others are people working in other functions such as operations, marketing, or technology who wanted to transition into risk.

The conversation often takes the form of a 30-minute coffee chat or a phone call. I am sure each person I talked to left with new information gained from the conversation. However, at the same time, they probably had even more questions if they were interested in learning more.

There are many resources online today about retail risk, but the information is still highly fragmented.

This book is meant to provide a more systematic view of the daily practices in retail risk - what kind of decisions get made, what the business objectives are, and how different components come together, from data to system to strategy.

Other Professionals Working in the Lending Ecosystem

This book covers a lot of the practices used by first line risk managers working within a lender.

However, if you happen to work in a non-lender business within the ecosystem, such as a fintech partner, system vendor, service provider, regulatory body, or recruiting agency, you might also find it beneficial to understand the risk management practices on the lender's side. With that knowledge, you can better design your products and services to help your institution work with your clients more effectively.

Lastly, this book is written based on my experience in the U.S. and Canada. For markets with a credit infrastructure similar to that of North America, the contents presented in the book can probably be readily related to. However, even for emerging markets with a credit infrastructure that is still under development, I believe some concepts and principles remain relevant — as the essence of retail credit and risk management should remain the same even in different credit environments.

1.2 The Writing Approach of this Book

The length of the book

This book is meant to help the reader establish a quick overview of retail risk management practices, thus its length has been kept under 300 pages. In this way, you will be able to finish the book within a couple of weeks, if you spend just thirty minutes to an hour during your lunch break or in the evening.

The book is also meant to provide the business context for risk decisions. Thus, it could be used as pre-read material before you dive into a particular project, such as risk model development or risk system documentation.

There are extensive technical manuals and documentations about risk systems, risk models, and risk policies that might be hundreds of pages long. This book is by no means intended to replace those key documents; rather, this could serve as compact and complimentary reading material.

Once you have built up the foundational knowledge from this book, it will be easier to dive into those documents and focus on the specific information you want to research in further detail.

Simplified Examples

I would like to point out that, due to the brevity of this book, the constructed examples are very simple.

The decision elements listed are the most common ones. The sample strategies provided are the basic minimal versions — just meant to allow readers to grasp the concepts quickly and gain a basic understanding.

In reality, the simplest risk strategy would be more complicated than the examples provided here, while some could become very sophisticated.

Depending on portfolio size, composition of clientele, and the particular macro-economic environment at the moment, you will always be able to come up with new rules to refine the strategies.

The quantitative analysis will provide numeric evidence for designing new rules. As well, you can always use creativity to balance the needs from the risk team and the business team. Risk management is a discipline in which you can deploy both science and art to make sophisticated decisions.

1.3   Structure of the book

This book is organized into five main sections.

Section I provides an introduction to this book. After the conclusion of Chapter 1, Chapter 2 introduces the role of retail lending in the overall economy, why risk management is important, especially in unsecured lending, and typical risk organization structure.

Chapter 3 provides an overview of key risk scores, which are important building blocks of risk strategies. The development and monitoring of scorecards is also presented.

Section II will walk you through the beginning of a credit life cycle - origination. Chapters 4–6 introduce various origination channels, the origination process and strategy, as well as performance monitoring.

Section III continues along the credit life cycle. Chapters 7–12 cover the account management decision areas, from authorization to collections. Some chapters are only relevant to credit cards or lines of credit, while others are applicable to installment loans as well. Exhibit 1-1 provides a summary of the applicability of each chapter with main unsecured credit products.

Section IV consists of Chapters 13–15, which cover key infrastructure components of retail risk management: risk data, risk system, and fraud.

Section V, which includes Chapters 16–18, presents overall portfolio risk management. Chapter 16 covers some key concepts in portfolio risk management, while Chapter 17 goes over the common portfolio risk reports. Chapter 18 presents some ideas on how to manage a credit portfolio dynamically through a full business cycle.

Exhibit 1-1 Sections and Chapters in relation to Major Unsecured Credit Products

Sections and Tables	Credit Card	Line of Credit	Installment Loan	Overdraft
SECTION I INTRODUCTION				
Chapter 1. Introduction	-	-	-	-
Chapter 2. Retail Risk Management	x	x	x	x
Chapter 3. Risk Score	x	x	x	x
SECTION II ACCOUNT ORIGINATION				
Chapter 4. Origination Channel	x	x	x	x
Chapter 5. Origination Strategy	x	x	x	x
Chapter 6. Origination Performance Management	x	x	x	x
SECTION III ACCOUNT MANAGEMENT				
Chapter 7. Authorization	x	x		x
Chapter 8. Credit Line Increase	x	x		x
Chapter 9. Credit Line Decrease	x	x		x
Chapter 10. Collections	x	x	x	x
Chapter 11. Reissue	x			
Chapter 12. Portfolio Stimulation Campaign	x	x		
SECTION IV RISK INFRASTRUCTURE				
Chapter 13. Risk Data	x	x	x	x
Chapter 14. Risk System	x	x	x	x
Chapter 15. Fraud	x	x	x	x
SECTION V PORTFOLIO RISK MANAGEMENT				
Chapter 16. Portfolio Risk Management	x	x	x	x
Chapter 17. Portflio Risk Reports	x	x	x	x
Chapter 18. Manage through Business Cycle	x	x	x	x

Next, let's look at retail lending and retail risk management.

Chapter 2
Retail Risk Management

This chapter begins with an introduction to retail lending business in Section 2.1 — how retail lending is closely tied with the daily lives and important life events of consumers.

Then, Section 2.2 illustrates the profit model of retail lending using the credit card as an example. Also explained is why risk management is an important element of the calculation.

Section 2.3 covers the prevalent risk management structure within financial institutions, as well as the key stakeholders that a risk professional regularly interacts with.

2.1 Retail Lending Business

Retail Lending, also called Consumer Lending, is an important part of the overall economy. In developed economies, consumer spending usually is a large component of the GDP. In the U.S., for example, consumer spending as a percentage of GDP has gradually increased over the last 40 years to about 68%.

Exhibit 2-1 Consumer Spending as a Percentage of GDP in the U.S., 1980-2020

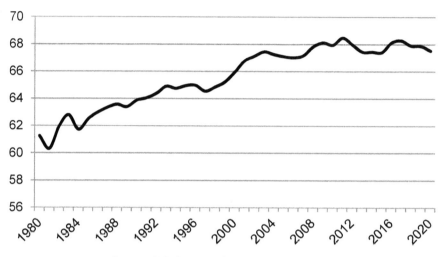

Source: U.S. Bureau of Economic Analysis[1]

A lot of consumer spending is facilitated with retail credit. For example, the credit card is a popular payment method in the U.S. and Canada, with an extensive acceptance network and incentive of various credit card reward programs provided by card issuers.

For the purchase of large ticket merchandise, such as furniture or jewelry, there are retail finance companies that provide 12-month or 24-month equal payment plans, often with low interest rate, which essentially makes the purchase much more affordable for consumers.

Retail lending is also closely associated with almost all of the consumers' major life events. Student loans help finance the cost of higher education. Car loans allow the consumer to own a vehicle, which is often required to commute to work. Mortgages fulfill the dream to own a property one calls home.

With the broad applicability of credit in the consumers' life, credit products have gained quite some growth over the years, even with some fluctuation.

Exhibit 2-2 depicts the change in the balance of major retail lending products in the U.S. over the past 17 years.

Exhibit 2-2 Balance of Retail Lending Products in the U.S., 2003-2020 (USD Trillion)

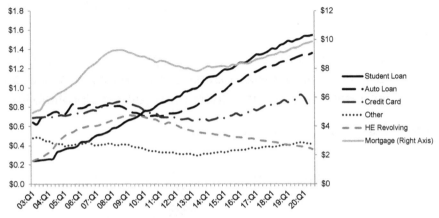

Source: Federal Reserve Bank of New York[2]

You can see that, after the impact from the 2008 great financial recession, which lasted until 2013, all types of consumer credit products have experienced growth, except for the home equity revolving product. Please note that mortgage, home equity revolving and auto are secured products and thus are not covered in this book.

As of Q3 2020, the total balance from consumer lending products reached $14.35 trillion, almost double the balance at the beginning of 2003. To put things into perspective, the total balance of consumer lending is about two-thirds of the U.S. GDP in 2019.

Such a large scale provides ample opportunities for various participants in the consumer lending ecosystem — from banks and credit unions to fintechs. How do lenders make money in this business? What is risk management's role in this line of business? Let's look at an example in the next section.

2.2 Retail Risk Management

Risk management is an important function in the retail lending business, as credit risk is inherently the largest controllable risk that lenders face. It helps to look at a simplified business model to understand risk's role.

Let's look at the credit card as an example, a product many people use on a daily basis. Exhibit 2-3 is compiled based on the Federal Reserve's annual report on credit card profitability.

Exhibit 2-3   Credit Card Profit Model

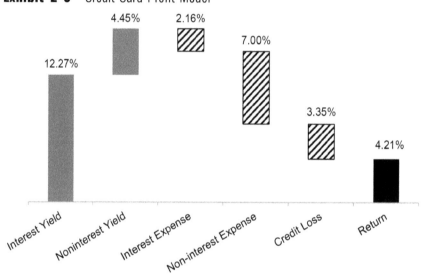

Source: Board of Governors of the Federal Reserve System[3]

As the exhibit shows, Total Yield is equal to Interest Yield + Non Interest Yield = 12.27% + 4.45% = 16.72%.

After deducting the Interest Expense of 2.16% and the Noninterest Expense of 7.00%, the portfolio has a return before credit loss equal to 16.72% – 2.16% – 7.00% = 7.72%.

The Credit Loss component of 3.35%, which is a reflection of risk, accounts for about 44% of return before taking risk into account, which is a fairly significant portion.

Thus, it is very important to manage the risk level down to within a certain range in order to make the portfolio profitable.

Suppose the credit loss rate doubles to 3.35% x 2 = 6.70%, then the final return of asset becomes a mere 7.72% – 6.70% = 1.02%.

If the loss rate becomes even higher, the portfolio quickly becomes unprofitable. That is exactly what happened in the 2008-2009 great financial crisis, the quickly rising loss rate made the credit card's return dwindle and reach a bottom of -5.33% in 2009 (see Exhibit 2-4).

Exhibit 2-4 Credit Card Return on Asset vs. Credit Loss Rate (%)

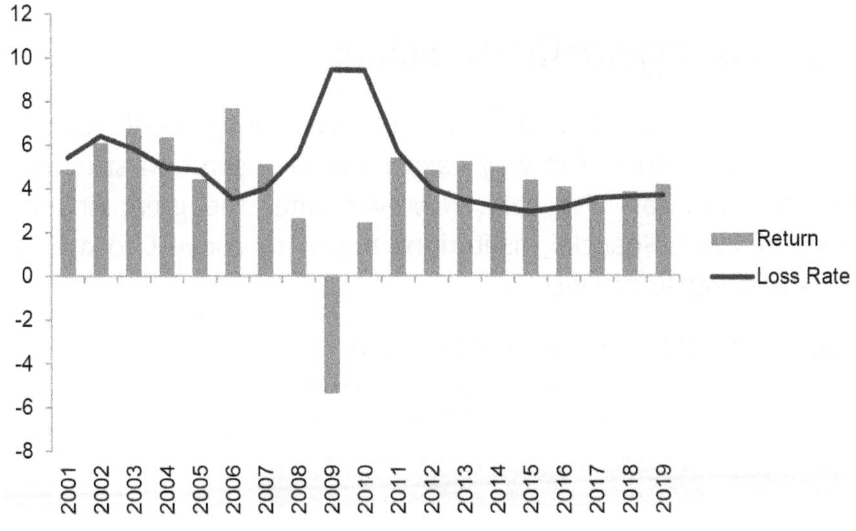

Source: Board of Governors of the Federal Reserve System[4]

Thus, it is important to manage a credit portfolio's risk level at a stable level. A rising risk level will quickly eat into the profitability of the business. A further increase in risk level would lead to financial loss, and sustained and heightened loss will impact the viability of a lender.

It is therefore important to have prudent risk management corresponding to the lender's business strategy.

For secured lending, such as a mortgage, the property is the collateral and can be sold through the foreclosure process to mitigate the bad debt.

For unsecured lending such as credit card and personal loan, there is no collateral to take as recourse if the borrower defaults on the loan. Thus, the risk of unsecured lending is relatively higher, and it is even more important to have prudent risk management practices.

Now that we understand the role of risk management in the retail lending business, let's look at how a risk team is organized and who the stakeholders are that the risk team interacts with on a regular basis.

2.3 Risk Organization Structure

The organization structure of the risk management team is evolving over time. The way each financial institution structures its risk team can also vary. However, after the great financial crisis of 2008, financial institutions began to convert to a three lines of defense model.

Exhibit 2-5 The Three Lines of Defense Model

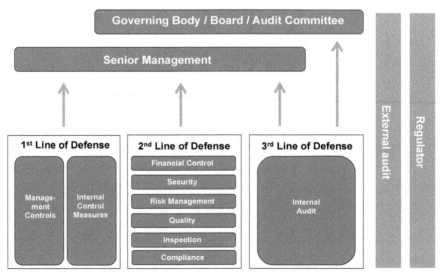

Source: The Institute of Internal Auditors[5]

The first line of defense is conducted by the line of business team. This broad team includes the first line of credit risk staff, who often reports with a dotted line to the head of the line of business. The first line of defense team has intimate knowledge of the products, customers, and processes, so this is where risk control and mitigation are best accomplished.

The first line risk management team makes day-to-day risk decisions. Scenarios, strategies, and performance monitoring related to these daily risk decisions comprise the main body of this book. The first line risk management team does not work in isolation — it works closely with a wide range of stakeholder groups in line of business and corporate functions.

Among the various teams within the second line of defense, there is a second line risk management team that provides oversight of first line team's risk decisions. This team is supposed to provide credible challenges to first line team's decisions. The idea is to have an additional pair of eyes to review risk decisions to ensure that the entire decision making process is a prudent one.

As the second line risk team will typically review the risk proposal and its related quantitative analysis, it does not need to have as many resources as the first line risk team. With that being said, some second line risk teams do perform their own risk analysis as a way to evaluate the proposal from the first line risk team.

The duties of third line of risk defense team are carried out by the internal audit team. Internal audit reviews the process and documentation from the first line and second line of defense teams to assess the overall effectiveness and adequacy of the risk management framework. The third line of risk defense team also ensures that proper validation is done and the appropriate effective challenge is being performed.

Ideally, the second line and third line risk teams should possess similar knowledge and experience as the first line risk team, if not more. In this way, an effective and credible challenge can be performed. However, this is not necessarily the case at some financial institutions, especially when the three lines of defense model was first introduced and there was a shortage of experienced risk talents.

External audit firms are hired by financial institutions to perform independent audits. There are also regulators, such as the OCC, the Fed, CFPB in the U.S., and OSFI in Canada. Regulators perform a regular review of the risk management practices of financial institutions under their jurisdiction, in order to make sure those practices are both compliant and prudent.

To date, the three lines of defense model has been widely adopted in the banking industry. The overall financial system is more resilient compared to the pre-2008 era, but the risk management framework continues to evolve.

Stakeholders of First Line Risk Management Team

Many of the topics covered in this book are what a first line risk management team is dealing with on a daily basis. In practice, many different aspects of risk management involve the interaction and collaboration with various internal and external stakeholders.

Exhibit 2-6 illustrates the different stakeholder groups that a first line risk management team typically interacts with.

Exhibit 2-6   Stakeholders of the First Line Risk Team

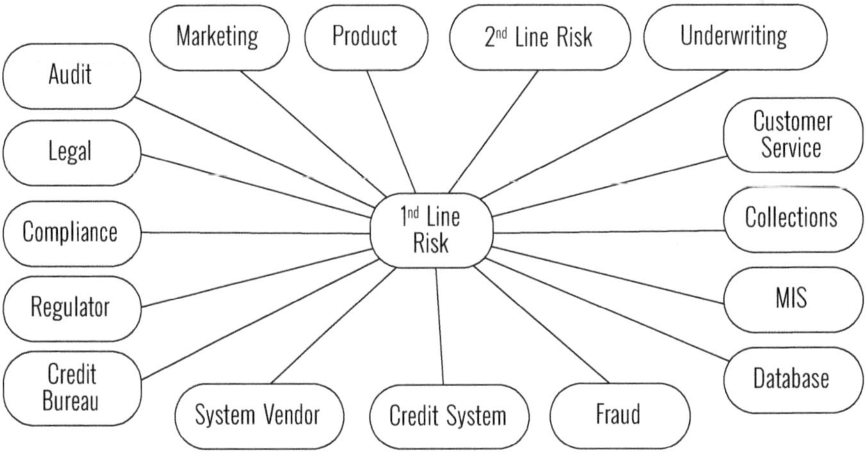

One group of internal stakeholders includes those who the first line risk team needs to collaborate with in order to implement risk strategies. Such stakeholders include the second line risk team, and underwriting, collections, credit system, and fraud staff.

The other group of stakeholders is on the business side. Their focus is more geared toward revenue generation and customer satisfaction. By design, the risk team's interactions with this group of stakeholders could have some natural tensions. However, such tension is necessary to ensure that the final risk decision is a balanced one between revenue and risk. Among this group of stakeholders are the product, marketing, and customer service departments.

Other internal stakeholders include those in control functions, such as audit, legal, and compliance staff. These groups will help ensure that your risk decisions and practices fully comply with legal clauses and regulations, and are robust enough to withstand the audit review.

Externally, besides regulators, there are credit bureaus and risk system/tool vendors who provide the basic yet important tools that risk professionals need to carry out their jobs on a daily basis.

Risk strategy is a high-touch decision strategy, as it often impacts customers in many ways, especially for unsecured revolving products such as credit cards. It is important for first line risk teams to maintain close working relationships with these diverse stakeholders, as you can gather feedback from different perspectives, some of which are a natural extension of the voices from customers.

The communication also serves as an opportunity for risk teams to learn many facets of daily operations beyond pure risk management. All of these will help you validate and further refine risk strategies and make comprehensive and balanced decisions.

With this introduction, you hopefully now have a good understanding of why risk management is an important function in retail lending and how the risk team fits into the overall organization structure.

Next, let's look at the key building blocks of risk management: risk scores.

Chapter 3
Risk Scores

Risk scores are important building blocks of all the risk strategies throughout the credit life cycle. There are many great books on risk scorecard development and risk modeling. This chapter provides an introduction from the score user's perspective.

Section 3.1 introduces some commonly used risk scores. Section 3.2 talks about the score development process and consideration. Section 3.3 lists several measures to monitor scorecards.

3.1 Common Risk Scores

This section lists some of the most commonly used scores for unsecured lending portfolios and how they are used in risk management practices.

3.1.1 Credit Bureau Score

A credit bureau score is widely used in credit decisions. As the first credit score was developed by Fair Isaac Company, many people simply refer to the credit bureau score as FICO score.

Over time, credit bureaus have actually developed their own scorecards and assign different score names, such as VantageScore[1], but some people get used to the generic name and just refer to all credit bureau risk scores as a FICO score. This is similar to people referring to all brands of tissue as Kleenex.

A credit bureau score typically ranks order the likelihood that an account will become 90+ days delinquent or a charge-off in the next 24 months. The range of the score is usually between 100 and 900. The higher the value of the score, the lower the risk posed by the borrower.

Exhibit 3-1 shows an illustrative score-to-odds relationship. In this example, a credit bureau score of 675 has 30:1 good/bad odds. As the score value increases, the odds will become larger, indicating lower risk.

Exhibit 3-1 Score-to-Odds Relationship

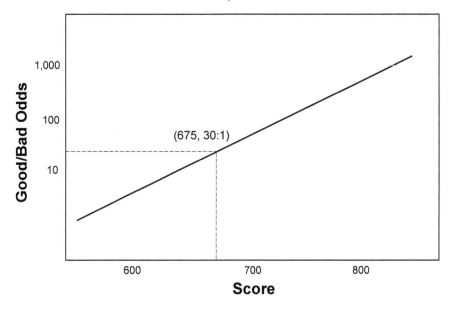

It should be noted that the score ranks order the performance of accounts in each score group. However, it cannot accurately predict which accounts will become bad.

The score is typically developed based on the national population that has a credit profile with the credit bureau.

As a credit bureau score encompasses all of the consumer's credit information, it is almost something that must be used in all credit decisions. A credit bureau score has wide applicability, in all products from credit card to mortgage and auto loan, across the entire credit life cycle, from origination to account management.

3.1.2 Application Score

An application score evaluates the risk of a credit application. It typically predicts the likelihood that an application will become 90+ days delinquent or a charge-off within the next 24 months.

As each lender and their unique credit products tend to attract different application populations, a custom score that is developed, based on their own application population, will better distinguish the risk vs. vendor risk score.

This custom score that is developed on the lender's application population is referred to as the "application score." Some companies may refer to their scores as custom origination scores or some other name, but their purposes are the same.

An application score is a main decision element used in account origination strategy for approval/decline decision and limit/loan amount assignment.

3.1.3 Bankruptcy Score

A bankruptcy score typically predicts the probability of an accountholder declaring bankruptcy within the next 24 months.

There are bankruptcy scores developed by credit bureaus based on the entire industry. Sometimes, a large credit portfolio chooses to develop its own bankruptcy score — because the score is developed on its own portfolio, the predictive power will usually be better than the industry-based version.

Bankruptcy scores can be used in both origination and account management strategies, such as authorization, CLI, and CLD.

3.1.4 Profit Score

A profit score, also known as a profit index, usually ranks an account's expected profitability during the next 12 months. An index from 1 to 10, for example, instead of the actual predicted profitability amount, is easy to implement in the risk system.

A profit score can be developed based on the overall industry or an individual portfolio.

The application of a profit score can be in origination and account management decision areas.

3.1.5 Behavior Score

For a revolving credit product, such as credit cards or lines of credit, there are ongoing credit decisions to be made after account origination. Behavior score is one main tool for evaluating the ongoing risk of the account and facilitating account management decisions.

For accounts that are current, or one or two cycles delinquent, a behavior score typically predicts the likelihood that the account will become bad (a charge-off or three or more cycles delinquent) within the next 6 months. For accounts already three or more cycles delinquent, a behavior score typically projects the total payment collected in the next 6 months as a percentage of the current balance.

If a credit portfolio has just recently been launched, there are industry behavior scorecards to use. As the credit portfolio grows and becomes mature, the lender can develop its own behavior scorecard, which tends to provide better lift in terms of predictive power.

Behavior score is typically used in account management decisions for revolving credit products, such as authorization, credit line management, collections, and reissue.

3.1.6 CLD Score

For revolving credit products, a lender needs to closely monitor the portfolio and identify those accounts whose risk levels have grown dramatically. Once an account's risk level becomes too high to support the existing credit limit, an action of credit line decrease (CLD) would be suitable to reduce the exposure to risk.

As an account's risk level can be determined by many factors from the internal behavior history to external credit holding and payment behaviors, a score is an effective way to identify high risk accounts without occupying a lot of decision elements in a risk strategy.

A CLD score typically evaluates the risk of an account in the ensuing 12–24 months, i.e., the likelihood that an account becomes 90+ days delinquent or a charge-off during the performance period.

A CLD score is usually a custom score developed for an individual portfolio. It is used specifically in the CLD strategy for revolving products.

3.1.7 Collections Score

Once an account becomes delinquent, a lender needs to determine what kind of collections action to assign to the account and when.

For accounts at different delinquency stages, different collection scores are used to facilitate collection decisions.

Early Stage

At early stage delinquency, a lender needs to know which accounts just need a gentle reminder vs. which ones need collection phone calls, in order to best allocate the collection resources.

An early stage collection score typically predicts the likelihood that an account less than 90 days delinquent will become current within the next three months.

If the score indicates that the probability of cure (becoming current) is high, a lender can give the account a few more days to see if it can self-cure or just send a gentle reminder. Otherwise, the lender can put the account in the dialer and initiate a phone call.

Late Stage

Once an account ends up in late stage, a lender's main objective is to stop the account from rolling forward and eventually becoming a charge-off. Thus, the efforts are geared toward collecting as much payment as possible from these accounts.

Thus, a late stage collection score typically evaluates the size of expected payments as a percentage of the balance within the next 3 to 6 months. The score helps identify accounts that are likely to pay the most, so they can be prioritized by collections operations.

Collection scores are typically developed for a specific industry, such as bank card or retail card; they can also be customized for a specific lender.

3.1.8 Fraud Score for Application

Fraud score for application evaluates the fraud risk of a credit application.

This is usually an industry scorecard. The score can be used to drive an approval/decline decision, as well as limit/loan amount assignment.

3.1.9 Fraud Score for Transaction

Fraud score for transaction evaluates the fraud risk of an authorization.

It is usually an industry scorecard, although a custom scorecard can be developed for large card issuers. The score is typically used in transactional fraud strategies, in combination with some other decision elements, to facilitate the decisions of approval, decline, and whether to place accounts in fraud queues for further investigation.

3.1.10 Small Business Risk Scores

Small business credit accounts have a set of risk scores similar to those of consumer accounts. The main difference is that the input variables of a small business risk score typically are a combination of small business attributes and personal attributes of the business owner.

This is due to the fact that many small businesses might not have full credit bureau files in the commercial credit bureau database, especially for those that are newly established. Thus, it is common to use the owner's personal credit attributes to compliment commercial records in order to get a good assessment of small business credit risk.

3.2 Scorecard Development Process

Do you need a (new) scorecard?

A score is a numeric representation of risk (or another particular metric) that you can use easily in a risk strategy. It can replace multiple decision elements and greatly simplify the strategy structure.

However, the ease of use does not come without cost. With the increased emphasis on model risk management post the 2008 financial crisis, all models, including scorecards, are subject to a great deal of scrutiny.

The thorough review applies to both model development and ongoing monitoring — sometimes it could become a fairly lengthy exercise. The additional time and resources needed to document and explain the scorecard should be weighed against the benefit.

Who should develop your new scorecard?

When it comes to the actual development of a new scorecard, you typically have the option to either develop it internally, or you can resort to external service providers such as FICO and credit bureaus.

Below are some reasons to support a lender to go with one or the other option.

The reasons to support using internal modeling resources:

☑ Besides modeling skills and experience, internal resources usually already possess intimate knowledge about the specific credit portfolio.

   ▶ Please note that this is not always true, given that a lender could have a complex organization structure, which could result in modeling a team that is further removed from the daily operations of a credit portfolio.

☑ The cost of scorecard development is lower than engaging an external service provider.

   ▶ There is still implicit opportunity cost, as the modeling resource can always work on alternative initiatives.

The reasons to support using an external modeling service provider:

☑ The external service provider has great modeling expertise in the specific area, cultivated from working with multiple clients over time. The output scorecard is likely to outperform the one developed by the internal team.

☑ The use of the output score has a large impact on the portfolio's P&L, thus the cost of scorecard development is relatively small compared with the potential financial gain.

☑ Internal resources are tied with other priorities already, and thus will not be able to work on the new scorecard development within the desired timeframe.

☑ The reputation and expertise of the external modeling service provider would help make the model vetting process easier.

Who should be involved?

It would be good to engage all the stakeholders of the scorecard early on during the model development process. Some typical stakeholders include the first line risk, first line business, second line risk, model vetting, legal, compliance, and credit systems teams. After the initial conversation, each stakeholder team can decide how closely they need to be involved and at what point.

This will help avoid the situation in which some questions and concerns occur at the last minute, which could cause rework and significantly delay the entire project.

3.3 Scorecard Monitoring

It is a good practice to regularly monitor the scorecard, in order to detect any issue during scorecard implementation or the possible deterioration of the scorecard over time.

Monitoring Reports

A few simple reports can be used for monitoring purposes if there is any large variation of score distribution from time to time. If there is, then further investigation can be conducted.

Score Distribution Change Report

Exhibit 3-2 shows the percentage change of account volume in each credit bureau score band. Such a graph provides a direct view of which score zone the account volume increases or decreases in, compared with the previous period.

Exhibit 3-2 Quarterly Score Volume Distribution Change

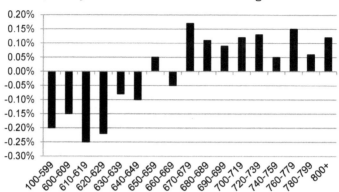

Score Migration Report

Besides understanding the before and after score distribution, it is also helpful to understand how accounts migrate among various groups.

Exhibit 3-3 shows how account distribution by score band has shifted from previous quarter to current quarter, by credit bureau score band. The lower-left area, where it is shaded, represents accounts with scores migrating downwards. These accounts need more attention, as the decrease in the score is a sign of growing risk.

Exhibit 3-3 Quarterly Score Migration

| | | Current Quarter | | | | | | |
		1-599	600-639	640-679	680-719	720-759	760-799	800+	Total
Previous Quarter	1-599	4.0	0.5	0.3	0.2	-	-	-	5.0
	600-639	0.3	7.5	0.3	0.2	0.1	0.1		8.5
	640-679	0.1	0.3	9.0	0.4	0.3	0.1	-	10.2
	680-719	-	0.2	0.4	13.5	0.4	0.3	0.2	15.0
	720-759	-	0.1	0.2	0.4	16.0	0.4	0.2	17.3
	760-799	-	0.1	0.3	0.3	0.4	17.5	0.4	19.0
	800+	-	-	0.2	0.3	0.4	0.5	23.6	25.0
	Total	4.4	8.7	10.7	15.3	17.6	18.9	24.4	100.0

Key Scorecard Monitoring Metrics

There are several commonly used metrics that measure the effectiveness of a scorecard. The values of these metrics in the most recent period can be compared with those in previous periods in order to see if there is any major deterioration.

Portfolio Stability Index (PSI)

The portfolio stability index is a numeric representation of the scorecard's stability in a portfolio. It is calculated as:

Sum of [(New weight — Old weight) x In (New weight/Old weight)]

for each score band.

Exhibit 3-4 shows an example of PSI calculation based on FICO Score. The old weight of each score band in Q1 '21 is referred to as column A. The new weight of each score band in Q2 '21 is referred to as column B. PSI is equal to the sum of (B-A) x In (B/A) for each score band.

Exhibit 3-4 Example of PSI Calculation

	Q1 ' 21	Q2 ' 21	Change	In(B/A)	PSI
FICO	% of Acct (A)	% of Acct (B)	(B-A)		
100-599	5.00%	4.80%	-0.20%	(0.04)	0.0001
600-609	2.00%	1.85%	-0.15%	(0.08)	0.0001
610-619	2.00%	1.75%	-0.25%	(0.13)	0.0003
620-629	2.00%	1.78%	-0.22%	(0.12)	0.0003
630-639	2.00%	1.92%	-0.08%	(0.04)	0.0000
640-649	2.50%	2.40%	-0.10%	(0.04)	0.0000
650-659	2.50%	2.55%	0.05%	0.02	0.0000
660-669	3.00%	2.95%	-0.05%	(0.02)	0.0000
670-679	4.00%	4.17%	0.17%	0.04	0.0001
680-689	5.00%	5.11%	0.11%	0.02	0.0000
690-699	5.00%	5.09%	0.09%	0.02	0.0000
700-719	6.00%	6.12%	0.12%	0.02	0.0000
720-739	7.00%	7.13%	0.13%	0.02	0.0000
740-759	8.00%	8.05%	0.05%	0.01	0.0000
760-779	9.00%	9.15%	0.15%	0.02	0.0000
780-799	10.00%	10.06%	0.06%	0.01	0.0000
800+	25.00%	25.12%	0.12%	0.00	0.0000
All	100%	100%			**0.0011**

The following guideline can be used to interpret the PSI value[2]:

✦ If the value is less than 0.1, the scorecard population is stable.

✦ If the value is between 0.1 and 0.25, the scorecard population has undergone a minor shift.

✦ If the value is greater than 0.25, then there has been a major shift in the scorecard population.

When the PSI indicates that the underlying population has experienced some kind of shift, you can look at other scorecard metrics and evaluate whether the scorecard still ranks ordering risk well, and then decide if any further action needs to be taken.

Kolmogorov-Smirnov (K-S)

The K-S statistic measures the degree to which the scorecard can separate good and bad account distributions. The value of the K-S statistic corresponds to the point of maximum percentage separation of the cumulative good and bad accounts along the score distribution.

Exhibit 3-5 K-S Statistic

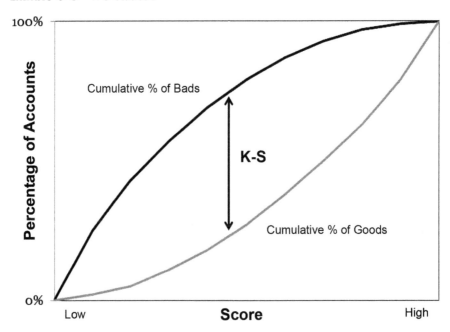

The following guideline can be used to interpret the K-S value percent:

✦ If the value is greater than 50, then the scorecard is strong.

- For a scorecard with a smaller volume, such as a delinquency scorecard, a value > 40 indicates the scorecard is strong.

✦ If the value is between 25 and 50, then the scorecard is moderate.

✦ If the value is less than 25, then the scorecard is weak.

Gini

The Gini coefficient is another commonly used metric to measure the discriminatory power of a statistical model, or stated another way, how effective the model is in differentiating between good and bad accounts.

The Gini coefficient is defined as the area under the Lorenz curve as a percentage of the area above the line of perfect randomness (the 45-degree line): A / (A+B). The higher the Gini value, the stronger is the scorecard.

Exhibit 3-6 Gini

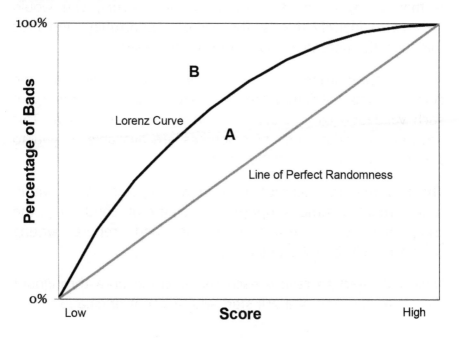

Divergence

The divergence statistic measures the separation between the distributions of good accounts vs. bad accounts. It considers the distance between the average of these two groups and the variances of the distributions.

It is calculated as:

$$Divergence = \frac{\left(Mean_{Goods} - Mean_{Bads} \right)^2}{\left[\dfrac{\left(Variance_{Goods} + Variance_{Bads} \right)}{2} \right]}$$

The higher the divergence statistic, the better a scorecard can separate the goods from the bads.

Frequency of Scorecard monitoring and Validation

Ideally, the scorecard monitoring is conducted on a monthly basis, right after the new scores become available. The reason is that if any issue of score production occurs, you would be able to identify that at the earliest opportunity, and thus minimize the potential loss caused by the issue.

If a comprehensive scorecard validation, as well as the corresponding validation report, is expected, the frequency of such validation can be set as *quarterly* or *semi-annually*. This depends on what kinds of resources are available to you to support the chosen validation frequency.

The fact that risk scorecards tend not to shift much within a few months' time supports the policy of conducting the comprehensive scorecard validation and report writing approximately 2 to 4 times a year.

Next, let's start to review each risk decision area throughout the credit life cycle. We will start with account origination.

SECTION II
ACCOUNT ORIGINATION

Chapter 4
Origination Channel

Overview

A credit application can be submitted from a bank's branch or a partner retailer's store. It can also be mailed in or submitted by phone to the lender's call center. With the boom of technology, more applications are now submitted via the Internet.

The applications associated with these different channels have different credit characteristics and thus possess different levels of risk. In practice, they are often managed with different strategies. Specifically, different channels have different decision strategies, limit strategies, and fraud strategies.

In this chapter, the following origination channels will be introduced and their unique characteristics will be highlighted:

- ☑ Prescreen
- ☑ Preapproval
- ☑ Branch and Store
- ☑ Internet
- ☑ Mail and Phone

4.1 Prescreen

Prescreen refers to the process in which a lender checks prospects' credit bureau files first and determines which ones are eligible for their credit product. Then solicitation offers are sent out to qualified prospects.

If a prospect responds to the solicitation and applies for credit, the application will go through the account origination decision process.

This is a very popular account acquisition approach in the U.S., especially for credit card and personal loans, because lenders are allowed to screen against the full nationwide credit bureau database including those who are not their customers.

Consider that there are more than 200 million[1] prospects to screen and target. That is one of the reasons that the consumer lending market in the U.S. is very competitive - lenders can target each other's customers and woo them away with all kinds of enticing offers.

Preapproved or not?

In practice, these solicitation offers in the U.S. are often presented to consumers as "preapproved," in the sense that the prospects get screened against the lender's origination strategy and would have been approved at the very moment of screening.

However, there will be a time lag from the screening to the final application submission. How long the lag is depends on how fast the lender can get the offers out to consumers and how long it takes for these consumers to respond and submit applications.

During the time lag, the consumer's credit situation could change, even though the vast majority usually have a stable credit in the short term. Thus, you would still have a small percentage of applications that are declined.

Because the offer is not 100% guaranteed, "prescreened" or "prequalified" would be more accurate names for this channel.

A prescreened application still needs to go through the credit policy, decision strategy, limit/loan amount strategy, and fraud strategy.

Credit Policy

The lender's credit policy should have been used during the prescreening process before the solicitation offer goes out. To play it safe, the application sent in response to the prescreen offer should still go through the same credit policy. This would capture any negative information that had recently surfaced, such as too many inquiries in recent days or a new charge-off tradeline.

Decision Strategy

Because the prospects have been prescreened, the decision strategy could be simpler compared to the one used under a regular channel.

The main objective is to make sure that there is not too much credit deterioration from the time of the prescreen to the time of the application. This can be verified by checking the latest credit bureau score and selected credit attributes.

Sometimes an issuer is wary of a potentially negative experience if a prescreen prospect responds to the solicitation but gets declined due to their score drifting downward, even by a few points.

In this case, the score cut-off used at the time of list generation can be set a bit higher than the score cut-off set in the actual decision strategy.

For example, a lender has a minimum credit bureau score requirement of 660 in its decision strategy. In this case, the minimum credit bureau score used at prescreening can be set at 680.

If a prospect's score has dropped from 680 at prescreening to 670 at application, it still will be approved because 670 is above 660 — the minimum score required.

Limit/Loan Strategy

For approved prescreen applications, a lender could just use the same limit/loan strategy as that which is used for a regular channel. There usually is no need to be creative.

Fraud Strategy

Because there are synthetic credit files created by fraudsters or prescreen mails could be intercepted, there is a real likelihood that fraudulent applications could come in along with legitimate ones.

Thus, it is important to have the prescreen application go through all the fraud checks. It is also a good idea to avoid some geographic areas (aka "hot spots") based on the lender's recent fraud experience. This requires close collaboration with the lender's fraud team.

Flexible Targeting

With the vast number of prospects available for prescreen — there are more than 200 million consumer credit files in the U.S. — a lender has a lot of flexibility to decide which prospects to target.

From geographic area to existing debt level, from housing status to risk scores, lenders can leverage multiple attributes to design various prescreen campaigns that can best utilize their budgets and achieve their business objectives.

Offer Delivery Channels

A prescreen offer traditionally is delivered by direct mail. With the rapid development of digitalization, direct mail is surprisingly still an effective way to acquire accounts — or at least was, prior to the pandemic in 2020. Consumers do open mail from various lenders, especially when some of them are on the lookout for new credit products and services.

If a reliable email address is available, this can also be deployed. The cost of email is much cheaper compared to traditional direct mail. However, given the amount of emails that consumers receive today, the offer might be buried among hundreds of other solicitation emails or even end up in the junk mail folder.

Nevertheless, a lender should always test email vs. mail delivery channels, in order to find the most effective way to attract applications and acquire new accounts.

Offer Response Channels

For a prescreen campaign, the lender usually provides several ways for prospects to submit the application so they can use the manner they are most comfortable with.

A lot of consumers nowadays would like to respond via the Internet. Thus, a link to the prescreen application site should be included in the solicitation offer that is mailed or emailed.

Some consumers would like to use the traditional method of mailing the application in. The issuer usually fills in the consumer's name and address on the application form to minimize the time they need to complete the form. A return envelope with paid postage would be convenient for the consumer as well.

Some consumers still like to talk to agents in real-time at a call center, as they might have questions about the offer. Thus, a phone number is also provided on the prescreen offer. The lender's call center should get prepared when a large prescreen campaign goes out, as the phone continues to be an essential channel to receive the application.

Prescreen of Internal Customers

Although prescreen is mostly performed against the large volume of external prospects available in the U.S., the same concept also applies to a lender's internal customers.

Actually, with additional information available from existing lending and deposit products, a lender can better assess a prospect's risk.

The decision strategy and limit/loan amount strategy can be adjusted for these internal customers, especially if it is an ongoing initiative to prescreen an existing customer base and cross-sell new loans.

Also, because the customer identification process has already been completed, the fraud strategy can be lighter.

4.2 Pre-approved

In Canada, where prescreen against non-customers is not allowed, the pre-approved approach is a popular way for full-service banks to cross-sell to existing customers and book new credit accounts.

Example 4.1 explains how a bank used the preapproved program to cross-sell credit cards to existing customers.

Example 4.1 Cross-sell of Preapproved Credit Card

A full-service bank provides the full range of consumer lending products, including credit cards, auto loans, and mortgages. Through customer level analysis, the bank found that only 15% of its mortgage and auto loans customers have a credit card from the bank, which lagged behind the industry level according to a benchmark report. In this case, the other 85% of mortgage and auto loan customers presented an excellent opportunity for the bank to cross-sell the bank's credit card.

Using the credit bureau score and attributes obtained on mortgage and auto loan customers, the bank was able to conduct a risk analysis of the 85% of the customers with no card. The performance on the mortgage and car loan provided additional information to help evaluate the customer's credit worthiness. With this analysis, the bank was able to identify a population of 200,000 to whom the credit card offer could be safely extended to.

A monthly preapproved program was later developed to target qualified customers via multiple channels. The bank successfully added 20,000 credit card accounts in the 12 months after the preapproved program was launched.

This form of pre-approved is different from its cousin south of the border in the sense that it is really meant to be a firm offer. When a preapproved offer is presented to the customer, if the customer accepts it, a new credit card account will be opened and the plastic will be shipped out. There is no further application to be submitted for the customer and there is no credit bureau pull.

Final Check

Of course, there is a final check, just in case something unfavorable happens after the list of the preapproved prospects is generated. Usually, the check is on the performance of the customer's existing credit product.

In Example 4.1, if a customer's mortgage or car loan becomes delinquent, this information would typically disqualify the preapproved offer.

Presentation and Fulfillment Channels

Canadian banks, which are all full-service banks, can take an "omnichannel" approach — leveraging all channels they have — to present the offers. These channels include direct mail, call center, email, online message, branch, and ATM.

The potential customer can be presented to via multiple channels during the period that a preapproval offer is valid. All the customer needs to do is to say "Yes" to the offer, or click a "Yes" button and the new credit card account will be opened. Nice and easy.

4.3 Branch and Store

Bank Branch

A branch network is important for lenders, as it allows them to serve consumers who still need face-to-face interaction.

Besides prescreen and preapproval, a branch is another major channel for credit applications to come in, especially if the lender has an extensive branch network.

With in-person interaction and the likelihood that the customer who goes to a branch probably already has some other products with the lender, the quality of in-branch applications is usually decent.

It is always good if another credit product can be marketed to an existing customer. A consumer with multiple products is usually more engaged with the lender, likely to use the products more often, and thus bring in more revenue.

Retail Store

For retail credit cards, the store is the paramount channel. Similar to bank branches, retail stores are where there is more foot traffic.

Often combined with rich discount offers from the retailers, credit offers have good acceptance rates at retailers' checkout counters. Over time, retailers and lenders have developed a quick application and decision process right at the POS (point of sale) terminal, also known as instant credit. This leads to the conversion of retail customers into millions of credit customers every year.

Because retail customers are applying for the credit right at the checkout counter with the merchandise in hand, it is crucial to have a high approval rate for in-store credit applications.

If the customer's credit application is declined in front of many other people in the checkout line, the negative experience might mean that this is the customer's last visit to the store, which is the last thing a retailer wants to see.

Thus, lenders behind retail credit programs all strive to achieve maximum approval rate for in-store credit applications, within the portfolio's risk appetite. That is why some retailer portfolios could see an approval rate in the mid-80s, while some banks can get by with an approval rate in the mid-50s.

4.4 Internet

The Internet has become an increasingly important channel of credit acquisition with the advancement of technology. It is where a lot of consumers spend time and it is convenient to submit the application when in front of a screen, without the need to even leave one's seat.

Online personal loan, for example, was booming after the 2008 Great Recession, with its streamlined easy-to-apply process over the Internet.

At the same time, the Internet exposes the lenders to fraud risk, as it does not require a physical interaction such as that which occurs in a branch or a retail store (although fraud does happen in these channels as well). The prevalence of identity theft and synthetic IDs being issued in recent years further exacerbates the fraud issue for lenders.

To address the high risk from Internet applications, lenders usually adopt more stringent origination strategies compared with other channels. This is achieved via tactics such as:

☑ Special digital identification and authentication tools

☑ Higher credit score cutoffs in decision strategy

☑ Higher fraud score cut-off

☑ Lower credit limit assignment

4.5 Mail and Phone

Without solicitations from lenders, consumers can still submit credit applications via traditional postal mail or phone.

With the growing trend toward digitalization, the volume of applications from these two channels is continually diminishing these days.

However, there are always some applicants who prefer to mail out paper forms or talk to a live agent over the phone, and thus these channels are here to stay.

Lenders do need to keep these options available in order to satisfy the needs of all potential customers.

Summary

As a risk professional, you will want to work closely with a business partner to understand the business' strategy and then design your origination strategies accordingly.

As applications coming through various channels have different characteristics and risk profiles, you should manage the origination strategies for each channel according to the aspects of each one.

Besides channels, what goes into the consideration of the strategy also includes approval rate, application process, the customer experience, and risk appetite.

Chapter 5
Origination Strategy

Once a credit application is submitted through a particular channel, it will go through a series of evaluation steps that have been set up in the origination strategy. If the application is not rejected at any of the steps, it will be approved and a new credit account will be established.

As the very first decision area in the credit life cycle, account origination is important for both risk management and business. Letting risky applications come into the book will cause the credit portfolio to incur loss at a later stage, as the extended loan cannot be repaid by the borrower.

At the same time, account origination brings new blood into a credit portfolio. A steady and healthy origination volume is vital for the organic growth of the portfolio.

5.1 Origination Process

As the simplified Exhibit 3-1 illustrates, once a credit application is submitted, the first step is to send the applicant's identification information to a credit bureau in order to obtain the applicant's credit report.

Exhibit 5-1   Credit Application Process

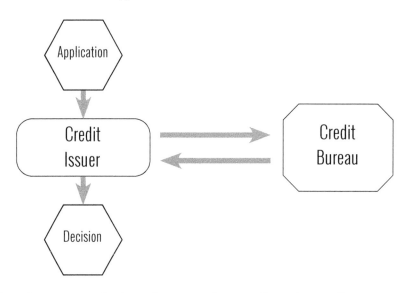

For the vast majority of cases, the applicant's credit report can be located and the report and key credit attributes will then be sent back to the credit issuer for further processing. Otherwise, the fact that no credit file is found (also known as "no hit") will be provided to the credit issuer.

Once the credit issuer receives the credit file search result, it will rely on a set of pre-defined policies and strategies to make a decision as to whether to approve or decline the application; if approved, how much of a credit limit (for revolving accounts) or loan amount (for installment products) to grant.

Section 5.2 provides an introduction to the credit bureau search process. Sections 5.3–5.6 break down the decision rules on the credit issuer side into several major components:

- ☑ Credit Policy
- ☑ Decision Strategy
- ☑ Limit/Loan Strategy
- ☑ Origination Fraud Strategy

5.2 Credit Bureau Process

Connection with the Bureau

Due to the high volume nature of the retail credit business, the credit check (also known as the credit bureau pull) is usually performed within a matter of seconds through a system-to-system connection. This automatic process is a must-have for lenders, allowing them to handle a large volume of retail applications, including those from consumers and small businesses.

The world's largest credit bureaus for consumers and businesses include Equifax, Experian, and TransUnion. Dun & Bradstreet, or D&B, is another major credit bureau focusing on businesses only.

Bureau Preference Table

In the U.S, national lenders usually have their preferred credit bureaus set at the state or zip code level, in consideration of each bureau's strength in a particular geographic area. A sample bureau preference table is provided in Exhibit 5-2. Some lenders even use a tri-bureau merged credit report in order to leverage all available credit information on the consumer.

Exhibit 5-2 Sample Bureau Preference Table

U.S. State	Equifax	Experian	TransUnion
Alabama	x		
Arizona			x
Arkansas		x	
California	x		
...	...	...	...
Virginia			x
Washington		x	

Bureau Matching Logic

The logic a credit bureau uses to identify and match an application with the bureau's consumer credit database is based on personal identification information such as:

- ☑ Social Security Number (SSN) in the U.S. / Social Insurance Number (SIN) in Canada
- ☑ Name
- ☑ Current and previous addresses
- ☑ Date of birth
- ☑ Phone number

A credit issuer can choose which matching rules to use. For example:

- ☑ Name + SSN/SIN
- ☑ Name + address + phone number

Bureau Matching Rate

For a typical credit issuer, the matching rate of applications, also known as the "hit rate," against a major credit bureau usually is around 90%.

The unmatched application or "no hit" could be due to the fact that the consumer's credit records did not get reported into that particular credit bureau, or the consumer has not established any credit in the market — a so-called "new to credit." Typical examples of new to credit applications are a student or an immigrant who does not have any credit product in the market yet.

Because there is a small percentage of the population whose credit records only get reported into one credit bureau and not the others, it is beneficial for a credit issuer to add a secondary bureau.

Primary Bureau vs. Secondary Bureau

The credit bureau that the credit inquiry is first sent to is called the "primary bureau" for the lender. It typically receives most of the lender's origination business.

The applications that get a no-hit from the primary bureau can be immediately sent to another credit bureau, thus referred to as the secondary bureau, if such an arrangement is in place.

With the dual-bureau process, the vast majority of applications should be able to get a hit with one of the bureaus. The credit bureau file and credit attributes are the very foundation for lenders to perform credit evaluations.

Origination Strategy

Once the credit bureau search result is returned, a credit application will typically go through the following major components in the origination decision engine:

☑ Credit Policy

☑ Decision Strategy

☑ Limit/Loan Strategy

☑ Application Fraud Strategy

5.3 Credit Policy

In the account origination process, a credit policy usually refers to a set of policy rules that determine which applications the credit issuer will consider and then continue through the rest of the adjudication steps, versus which ones will be declined up front.

The typical credit policy is developed around the following scenarios:

☑ Foreign Nationals such as foreign workers or foreign students

▸ A bank only focusing on the domestic market might restrict extending credit to foreign nationals.

▸ A subsidiary of an international bank will probably be open to selected foreign nationals.

☑ Recent derogatory records such as a charge-off, bankruptcy, or collections items.

☑ No hit — the application does not have a hit with any existing file at the credit bureau(s).

▸ Although it is always safe to decline a "no hit," among the no hits there is also the "new to credit" population, which includes students just reaching legal age to apply for credit or new immigrants who have just arrived in the credit market. These are opportunities to become the first lender to establish a relationship with these new-to-credit customers.

☑ Thin file — the applicant has very few credit tradelines, perhaps just 1 or 2, in the credit file.

☑ New file — the credit file has only recently been established, perhaps within the last 6 months.

☑ Recent delinquencies — there are delinquent tradelines that have been reported to the credit bureau recently.

☑ Recent inquiries — there are too many recent credit inquiries, in past 6 months, for example.

Examples of credit policies include the following (they often come in as exclusions or decline rules):

☑ Decline if there was a charge-off tradeline in the last 24 months.

☑ Decline if there was a non-charge-off derogatory tradeline in the last 24 months.

☑ Decline if the applicant is not a citizen or permanent immigrant.

☑ Decline if the applicant had a previous $ CO with the credit issuer.

☑ Decline if the applicant has <=2 trades.

Credit Policy vs. Credit Strategy

Some people use the two terms "Credit Policy" and "Credit Strategy" interchangeably, but I believe these two terms are best distinguished from each other.

Credit policy refers to the key rules that usually remain for the long term. It does not mean that the credit policy should always be set in stone, but the objective of the credit policy is to make it remain for an extended period, such as a few years or even an entire business cycle.

A credit policy should be formally documented in the lender's policy document.

Credit strategy is something that the first line of risk team can proactively adjust based on the changing economic environment, portfolio performance, and business needs.

For example, an application with FICO>720 will qualify for a premium credit card and will receive a credit line of no less than $10,000. This is considered a credit strategy.

If, 6 months later, the risk and business teams want to grow the premium card volume by lowering the cutoff to FICO 700 and assigning the limit starting at $8,000, this would be a credit strategy change.

5.4 Decision Strategy

If an application passes all the origination credit policies, it will go to the next component in the decision engine — decision strategy. In this step, further logic is applied to determine if the application is qualified for approval.

Next, let's take a look at some typical decision elements (also known as decision variables or decision keys) used in a credit decision strategy. A simple example of a decision strategy using these decision elements will also be presented.

Credit Bureau Score

Credit bureau score is the credit risk score provided by the credit bureau, calculated based on the credit file maintained for the applicant at the bureau.

Application Score

An application core is the credit risk score developed based on a lender's application population only.

A classic way to deploy an application score is to use it along with the credit bureau score in a dual matrix fashion.

Suppose the actual 24-month $ charge-off rate performance of a representative sample of credit card applications is as shown in Exhibit 5-3. The convention is that a high score value means low risk. That is why you see that lower $ charge-off rates are associated with the lower ranges for both scores.

Exhibit 5-3   24-month $ Charge-off Rate by Dual Score Matrix

		Application Score				
		1 - 599	600 - 699	700 - 799	800 - 899	900 +
Credit Bureau Score	1 - 599	30%	25%	20%	16%	14%
	600 - 639	20%	15%	12%	8%	6%
	640 - 679	16%	12%	8%	6%	4%
	680 - 719	12%	8%	6%	4%	3%
	720 +	10%	6%	4%	3%	2%

If the lender decides to accept any application with a 24-month $ charge-off rate within 8%, the cells with a high credit bureau score and a medium application score, or a high application score and a medium credit bureau score, will be approved, as shown in Exhibit 5-4.

Exhibit 5-4   Origination Decision Strategy by Dual Score Matrix

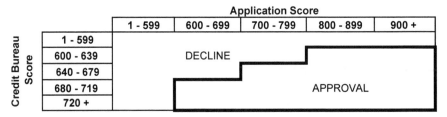

In reality, the strategy design is not purely based on the $ charge-off rate. Besides risk performance, application volume, profitability at the cell level, and overall application approval rate, all could factor into the consideration.

Bankruptcy Score

The bankruptcy score usually predicts the likelihood of the applicant declaring bankruptcy within the next 24 months. Similar to a risk score, usually the higher the score value, the lower the risk of bankruptcy.

Because bankruptcy is a rare event, the score is usually highly concentrated on the right, which means most of the population has high scores that represent a low bankruptcy risk[1] (see Exhibit 5-5).

A bankruptcy score that is below a certain cut-off can be declined immediately. For example, an issuer decides to decline all applications with a bankruptcy score of 600 based on analysis, concluding that this segment carries too much bankruptcy risk and is not profitable.

Exhibit 5-5 Distribution of Bankruptcy Score

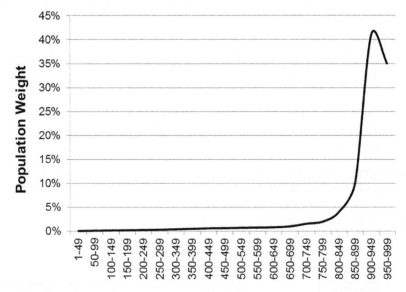

In addition to the minimum score cut-off, the bankruptcy score can also be used to drive the credit limit/loan amount assignment.

Not every credit issuer uses bankruptcy score as they need to justify its use by seeing that the incremental benefit will outweigh the cost. Usually, a credit portfolio with a deeper risk appetite (relatively higher credit risk) can better justify the use of a bankruptcy score.

5.5 Limit/Loan Strategy

If an application passes the decision strategy, it will enter the next module of limit strategy for revolving credit. In this section, we will use limit strategy for credit cards as an example.

For installment loans, the strategy to evaluate the loan amount and term is based on a similar concept.

5.5.1 No Ability-to-Pay Requirement

In Canada, there is no ability-to-pay requirement for credit cards. Thus, it is not necessary to use the debt-to-income ratio or residual income in a credit card origination strategy. The limit assignment can be achieved by using the same dual score matrix with the credit bureau score and the application score.

In the limit assignment table example in Exhibit 5-6, the lowest risk segment application score of 900+ and a credit bureau score of 720+ is assigned with the highest limit of $12,000. With lower scores, which indicate higher risk, the limit assigned decreases accordingly.

Exhibit 5-6 Origination Limit Assignment Table

		Application Score				
		1 - 599	600 - 699	700 - 799	800 - 899	900 +
Credit Bureau Score	1 - 599	DECLINE				
	600 - 639				$ 3,000	$ 5,000
	640 - 679			$ 3,000	$ 5,000	$ 8,000
	680 - 719		$ 3,000	$ 5,000	$ 8,000	$ 10,000
	720 +		$ 5,000	$ 8,000	$ 10,000	$ 12,000

Besides the credit bureau score and application score, the bankruptcy score can be utilized to assign a lower limit to those with a relatively lower bankruptcy score. Thus, the $ loss due to bankruptcies can be managed down, as compared to the limit assignment strategy above that does not make use of the bankruptcy score.

Exhibit 5-7 illustrates how the bankruptcy score is used. The applications with a bankruptcy score below 600 are declined. Those with bankruptcy scores 600-899 are approved, but with lower limits. The rest of the applications with bankruptcy scores of 900 and above are approved with regular limits.

Exhibit 5-7   An Example of Using the Bankruptcy Score in the Decision and Limit Strategy

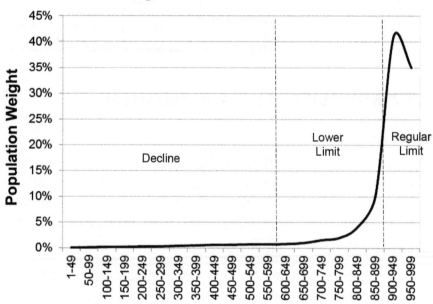

Exhibit 5-8 and Exhibit 5-9 show examples of the two sets of different limit assignments for high bankruptcy score and low bankruptcy score segments.

Exhibit 5-8   Origination Limit Assignment Table, Bankruptcy Score >= 900

		Application Score				
		1 - 599	600 - 699	700 - 799	800 - 899	900 +
Credit Bureau Score	1 - 599					
	600 - 639		DECLINE		$ 3,000	$ 5,000
	640 - 679			$ 3,000	$ 5,000	$ 8,000
	680 - 719	$ 3,000	$ 5,000	$ 8,000	$ 10,000	
	720 +	$ 5,000	$ 8,000	$ 10,000	$ 12,000	

Exhibit 5-9   Origination Limit Assignment Table, Bankruptcy Score 600-899

		Application Score				
		1 - 599	600 - 699	700 - 799	800 - 899	900 +
Credit Bureau Score	1 - 599					
	600 - 639		DECLINE		$ 1,500	$ 2,500
	640 - 679			$ 1,500	$ 2,500	$ 4,000
	680 - 719	$ 1,500	$ 2,500	$ 4,000	$ 5,000	
	720 +	$ 2,500	$ 4,000	$ 5,000	$ 6,000	

5.5.2 With Ability-to-Pay Requirement

CARD Act

Upon review of the 2008 Great Financial Recession, one lesson learned in the U.S. was that the extension of credit should not be unattached to a consumer's ability to pay the overall debt. Thus, an ability-to-pay requirement[2] was introduced with the CARD Act, enacted in 2009.

For credit extension at the time of origination or credit line increase (which we will cover in Chapter 8), the credit card issuer needs to adopt one of the following ways to consider a consumer's ability to repay the debt:

☑ Debt-to-income ratio

☑ Debt-to-asset ratio

☑ Residual income after paying the debt

Debt-to-Income (DTI) Ratio

Calculation of the DTI Ratio

To calculate the DTI with a new credit card, the following data elements are needed:

- ☑ **Income:** this is the self-reported income that a consumer provides on the credit application.
- ☑ **Housing Expense:** this is also provided by a consumer on the application, whether as a homeowner or renter. For the homeowner, to be cautious, the housing expense provided by the consumer can be compared to the monthly mortgage payment retrieved from the credit bureau, and the larger of the two can be used.
- ☑ **Monthly Payment with Existing Debt:** this can be found in a consumer's credit bureau file. There, an attribute will already have been calculated, which includes all of the consumer's non-mortgage debt payments in a month.
- ☑ **New Credit Line:** the CARD Act requires a card issuer to assume that the full credit line will be used on Day 1. The additional monthly debt occurred with the additional credit line associated with new credit card (if approved) needs to be added to the monthly debt for DTI calculation.

First, the estimated payment from the proposed credit line is calculated, with the assumption of a fully drawn limit. The payment from the new credit card is calculated using:

*New credit line * (APR/12 + 1%)*

The APR is the retail annual percentage rate assigned to the new credit card per pricing strategy. The 1% refers to the principal portion of the monthly payment, which is often used by lenders to ensure the overall credit card balance is being paid down each month.

Second, calculate the new monthly debt with the incremental payment from the new credit card. This monthly debt also includes the housing expense:

*Monthly non-mortgage debt payment + Monthly housing expense +
New credit card monthly payment.*

Lastly, the DTI ratio is calculated as:

New monthly debt / Monthly income.

Debt-to-Income (DTI) Strategy

There are different ways to assign the maximum DTI ratios based on various application segments. Exhibit 5-9 presents an example where a credit card issuer assigns DTI ratios based on the applicant's annual income and credit bureau score.

Exhibit 5-10 Maximum DTI Table

Annual Income	Credit Bureau Score			
	600-639	640-679	680-719	720+
<$40K	45	60	65	70
[$40K, $60K)	50	65	70	75
[$60K, $80K)	55	70	75	80
[$80K, $100K)	55	70	75	80
$100K+	55	70	75	80

All the DTI ratios in the exhibit are meant as caps or upper bounds. The final approved credit line can make the consumer's new DTI lower or equal to the DTI cutoff value specified in the corresponding cell, but cannot go over it.

Please note that the maximum DTI ratios increase as credit bureau score and/or annual income increase. This is because a good credit bureau score demonstrates a strong credit management capability. The higher annual income usually indicates a higher amount of free cash flow. For example, one with an annual income of $100,000 and 80% DTI ratio will have a free cash flow of $100,000 x (1–80%) = $20,000, while one with an annual income of $40,000 and the same DTI ratio will have a smaller free cash flow of $40,000 x (1–80%) = $8,000.

If an assigned credit limit would make the new DTI go over the specified cap, the strategy will test the next lower limit, with

$1,000 less, for example. It will continue the iterative process until the assigned credit limit satisfies the DTI requirement.

Let's look at Example 5-1 to see how the final approved limit is determined under the ability-to-pay rule.

Example 5-1 Limit Assignment under the Ability-to-Pay Rule

A consumer with a monthly income of $5,000 just submitted an application for a credit card. The credit card issuer deploys the decision strategy, limit strategy, and debt-to-income (DTI) rule presented earlier in this chapter.

The applicant's monthly total of their housing expense and their existing monthly non-mortgage debt payment add up to a total of $3,750.

With an excellent application score of 910 and a solid credit bureau score of 730, the application passes through the decision strategy and qualifies for a maximum limit of $12,000, prior to undergoing the ability-to-pay check.

The credit card has a standard 18% APR, thus a new limit of $12,000 will increase the consumer's monthly debt by:

$$\$12,000 * (18\% / 12 + 1\%) = \$300.$$

The new monthly debt plus the housing expense for the applicant will be:

$$\$3,750 + \$300 = \$4,050.$$

The new DTI ratio is:

$$\$4,050 / \$5,000 = 81\%.$$

With an annual income of $60,000 ($5,000 * 12) and a credit bureau score of 730, the consumer has a maximum allowed DTI ratio of 80%, as per Exhibit 5-8. Since the new DTI ratio of 81% is over the maximum allowed DTI ratio, the credit limit has to be lowered to below $12,000.

Then, the origination strategy lowers the assigned credit limit by $1,000 to $11,000 and the ability-to-pay will be checked again. Following similar steps, the new DTI ratio with a $11,000 limit is 80.5%, still higher than the cap of 80%. The calculation of each item under different limits is summarized in Exhibit 5-11.

The origination strategy lowers the assigned credit limit by another $1,000 to $10,000 and the same check is performed. Now the new DTI ratio drops to 80%, which is the allowed maximum. Thus $10,000 is the final credit limit assigned.

Exhibit 5-11 Ability-to-Pay Check with Different Assigned Limits

Approved Limit	APR/12 + 1%	Monthly Payment	Existing Monthly Debt	New Monthly Debt	Monthly Income	New Debt-to-Income Ratio
$ 1,000	2.5%	$ 25	$ 3,750	$ 3,775	$ 5,000	75.5%
$ 2,000	2.5%	$ 50	$ 3,750	$ 3,800	$ 5,000	76.0%
$ 3,000	2.5%	$ 75	$ 3,750	$ 3,825	$ 5,000	76.5%
$ 4,000	2.5%	$ 100	$ 3,750	$ 3,850	$ 5,000	77.0%
$ 5,000	2.5%	$ 125	$ 3,750	$ 3,875	$ 5,000	77.5%
$ 6,000	2.5%	$ 150	$ 3,750	$ 3,900	$ 5,000	78.0%
$ 7,000	2.5%	$ 175	$ 3,750	$ 3,925	$ 5,000	78.5%
$ 8,000	2.5%	$ 200	$ 3,750	$ 3,950	$ 5,000	79.0%
$ 9,000	2.5%	$ 225	$ 3,750	$ 3,975	$ 5,000	79.5%
$ 10,000	**2.5%**	**$ 250**	**$ 3,750**	**$ 4,000**	**$ 5,000**	**80.0%**
$ 11,000	2.5%	$ 275	$ 3,750	$ 4,025	$ 5,000	80.5%
$ 12,000	2.5%	$ 300	$ 3,750	$ 4,050	$ 5,000	81.0%

Debt-to-Asset Ratio

The debt-to-asset ratio is usually used to evaluate applicants with passive income generated from financial assets instead of the traditional income sources. It is simply calculated as:

New monthly debt / Total assets.

Please note that the asset here usually refers to liquid assets only, such as funds in a checking account, savings account, or certificate of deposit. Other assets would also be counted, but usually with a discounted factor — assets such as stocks, bonds, and mutual funds, which could easily lose value at the moment the customer liquidates them.

In practice, instead of using debt-to-asset ratio directly, many lenders choose to estimate the income generated from assets and then use debt-to-income or residual income. The income is usually calculated with an assumed annual rate of return on eligible assets, or as an annuity based on eligible assets and an assumed asset depletion period.

Residual Income

Also known as monthly disposable income, monthly residual income is calculated as:

Monthly income — New monthly debt.

Residual income is presented as a minimum requirement in the origination strategy. This means that, to approve the new credit, the applicant needs to have at least this much money in order to cover basic living expenses, such as food, health, and transportation.

For example, a credit card issuer specifies the minimum residual income as being $500.

If the residual income under a particular credit limit is less than $500, the credit limit needs to be lowered until the new residual income can meet the minimum $500 requirement. Otherwise, the application will be declined.

5.6 Application Fraud Strategy

Credit products always attract fraudsters who pose as the owner of legitimate identification documents or even fabricate synthesized identities. Thus, it is important that an application passes a series of fraud checks.

Fraud is a very complex and quickly evolving area and probably warrants its own book to present an in-depth review. Due to the scope of this work, I will just mention a few typical components deployed in an application fraud strategy.

☑ Fraud alerts from the credit bureau
  ▸ Whether there is any key element on the application, such as phone number or address, reported as being associated with known fraud.

☑ Fraud score
  ▸ A numeric evaluation of the likelihood that this application is from a fraudster vs. a legitimate applicant.

☑ Digital fraud mitigation tools
   ▸ For applications coming from digital channels, there are
     different tools to evaluate the fraud risk based on the
     applicant's profile, device identity, and behavior analysis.

☑ Check against the internal fraud database
   ▸ Establishing whether the application has some elements
     associated with internally known fraud activities.

A more detailed introduction of these fraud mitigation tools
can be found in Chapter 15 Fraud.

5.7   Adverse Action Letter

As per regulations, the decision of an application usually must be
made within a certain number of days after a completed application
is received, such as 30 days in the U.S[3]. For all declined applications,
a letter needs to be sent to the applicant to explain the reason(s)
for the decline. This letter is called an adverse action letter.

Also included in the adverse action letter is the credit bureau
score that the lender obtained, the name of the credit bureau
the score was obtained from, as well as the contact information
of the credit bureau.

A credit bureau score usually comes with 4 score reason codes
explaining the top contributing factors to the score value.
There is a specific verbiage corresponding to each score reason
code, which is provided to the lender by the credit bureau as
part of the score documentation. The lender needs to display
the verbiages corresponding to the score reason codes on the
adverse action letter.

It is important to review the assignment of adverse action letters
to ensure that all the decline scenarios have the appropriate
letters assigned. It is also a good practice to review the
assignment and verbiage of letters every 12-24 months, in order
to make sure they are still compliant with the latest regulation
and consistent with the lender's current brand strategy.

Chapter 6
Performance Measurement of Origination

This chapter wraps up the section on origination with performance measurement. It first introduces the key metrics used at the time of origination. Then it covers the performance measurement of origination vintages. The concept of champion/challenger is covered at the end, which actually applies to all decision areas in the credit life cycle.

6.1 Performance Measurement at Origination

6.1.1   Origination Volume

Origination volume is a key metric closely monitored by both risk and business teams. The total volume can be broken down by a key characteristic to help understand the composition.

Exhibit 6-1 shows a sample origination volume report with a breakdown by origination channel. The graph shows that the monthly loan volume has been fluctuating month by month, but is generally stable. However, the volume of loans originated from the Internet has been growing steadily, possibly reflecting the change in customer behaviors.

Exhibit 6-1 Monthly Origination Volume by Channel

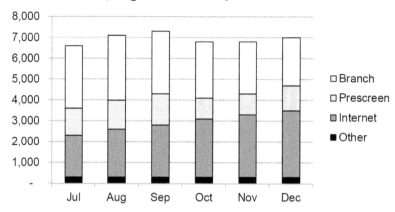

Besides origination volume by channel, other commonly used reports include:

☑ Origination Volume by Product

  ▸ For example, one card issuer has multiple card products to track: no fee card, cashback card, premium travel card, and secured card.

☑ Origination Volume by Loan Term

  ▸ For example, one personal loan lender has loans with 36-month and 60-month terms.

☑ Origination Volume by APR

  ▸ For example, an installment loan provider has different APR pricing for accounts with different risk levels.

6.1.2 Origination Risk

The risk level or credit quality of newly originated accounts (approved accounts) is important for the risk team to monitor.

One way to do this is to monitor the composition of the new origination by risk score. Exhibit 6-2 shows that the weights of mid-score and low-score bands have been growing over recent months. This is probably related to the fact that more accounts are originated over the Internet, which generally carries higher risk.

Exhibit 6-2 Monthly Origination Percentage by Credit Bureau Score

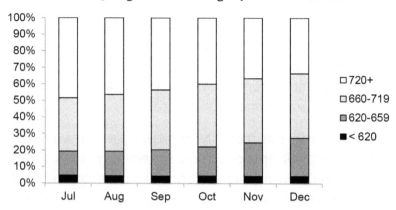

Other reports frequently used to track origination's risk include:

☑ Origination by Credit Grade
  ▸ Credit grade is a risk indicator typically driven by the credit bureau score and application score.

☑ Origination by Income Band

☑ Origination by Debt-to-Income Ratio Band

☑ Average Credit Bureau Score
  ▸ The average credit bureau score of new origination could fluctuate from month to month. However, if it steadily decreases over time, that means the credit quality of new accounts is deteriorating and is increasing the portfolio's overall risk. In this case, it should be further analyzed in order to understand the reasons behind the score decrease and what the appropriate mitigation action would be.

☑ Percentage of Originations with Low Credit Bureau Score
  ▸ For example, a lender tracks the percentage of its new accounts with FICO<620.

☑ Percentage of Originations with a Thin File
  ▸ For example, a lender allows the approval of credit for individuals with thin files, but doesn't want to see the proportion of thin file accounts increase too much. So, it tracks the percentage of thin file accounts among new origination every month.

6.1.3 Approval Rate

The approval rate of credit applications is an important metric that is closely monitored by both the risk and business teams. A higher approval rate means more approved accounts and more revenue opportunities down the road. It also implies a better overall experience for applicants.

Exhibit 6-3 shows the monthly approval rate of a credit card portfolio. The lower approval rates in recent months should be noted and analyzed further. If there are no recent changes in strategy, it could mean that the through-the-door applications have lower credit quality.

Exhibit 6-3 Monthly Approval Rate of Credit Applications

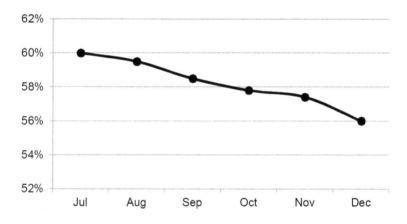

Through further investigation, the lender was able to confirm that the decrease in approval rate was due to the growing weight of Internet applications, which generally has a lower approval rate with lower credit quality.

To analyze the opportunity to increase the approval rate, a lender often looks at the reasons that applications are declined. Exhibit 6-4 shows that the major reasons for decline are a low credit score and not meeting the ability-to-pay requirement.

Exhibit 6-4 Reasons for Declining Applications

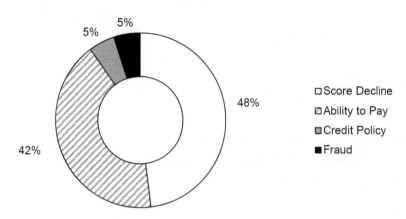

If a decline reason category experiences sudden growth, further research needs to be conducted to understand what has caused the change.

Similar analysis can be applied to the application deferral rate. An application deferral means there is no immediate approval or decline decision. The application is deferred to the underwriting team or fraud operations team for further manual review.

6.1.4 Branch/Dealer/Store Report

Origination reports can also be produced at the branch level for a bank. The origination volume is often put side by side with the plan number, so it is easy to compare the most recent progress against the initial plan.

Exhibit 6-5 shows a sample origination dashboard for a bank. The report clearly shows that branch 0002 is far ahead of achieving the new accounts goal for this fiscal year. An interview with the branch staff might reveal some best practices that other branches could learn from. On the other hand, it would be good to have a conversation with the officer of branch 0005 to understand what the challenge they are encountering and how to improve performance.

Exhibit 6-5   Branch Origination Dashboard at the Branch

Branch	# Applications	# Approved	Approval %	Avg Approved FICO	# New Accts in Plan	Actual/ Plan
0001	200	120	60.0%	729	135	89%
0002	260	155	59.6%	731	140	111%
0003	220	133	60.5%	728	140	95%
0004	190	118	62.1%	732	135	87%
0005	110	58	52.7%	730	80	73%

Depending on its business model, a lender might work with multiple retail dealers or stores. Similar reports can be generated for each dealer or store.

6.2 Performance Measurement of Origination Vintage

Vintage

Vintage is an important concept in the analysis of credit origination. It refers to new accounts that originated at the same time. For example, accounts originated in January 2020 can be referred to as the vintage of January 2020. Similarly, accounts originated from January 2020 to March 2020 can simply be referred to as the vintage of Q1 2020. Accounts originated throughout the entire calendar year of 2020 are referred to as the vintage of Year 2020.

Vintage Reports

Due to factors such as the macroeconomic environment, origination strategy changes, and the migration of customer behaviors, each origination vintage has its own unique performance.

Next, let's look at a few typical reports used to track the performance of origination vintages.

Vintage Delinquency Curves

As credit accounts always go through delinquency stages before becoming charge offs or losses, it is important to monitor the delinquency rates of each origination vintage to see whether the performance is within expectations or if there is an alarming trend.

Spot Delinquency Rate

One way to measure the delinquency rate is to measure the delinquency at a point of time against the balance at the same time, also known as a spot delinquency rate.

Exhibit 6-6 presents a simplified example — an origination vintage only has 10 accounts. For each account, the delinquency cycle in each month is captured.

Cycle 1 is equivalent to 1–29 days delinquent, Cycle 2 is equivalent to 30–59 days delinquent, and so on. A blank indicates that the account is current or non-delinquent in the given month.

Exhibit 6-6   Monthly Delinquency Status

Account ID	Jan '20	Feb	Mar	Apr	May	Jun	Jul	Aug	Sep	Oct	Nov	Dec
1001												
1002					1	2	3	2				
1003												
1004												
1005			1	2		1					1	
1006												
1007												
1008										1	2	3
1009												
1010												

In order to detect the delinquency early on, we use a 30-day plus unit rate as the metric, which is to measure the number of accounts delinquent 30 days or more as a percentage of the total number of accounts, which is 10.

As Exhibit 6-7 shows, account 1002 reaches 30+ days delinquency status (cycle 2+) in June, July, and August, but it cured or became current in the month of September. Thus, this account is only counted as 30+ delinquent account from June to August, but not in September and forward.

Exhibit 6-7 Spot Delinquency Rate

Account ID	Jan '20	Feb	Mar	Apr	May	Jun	Jul	Aug	Sep	Oct	Nov	Dec
1001												
1002						1	1	1				
1003												
1004												
1005				1								
1006												
1007												
1008											1	1
1009												
1010												
Total # 30+	0	0	0	1	0	1	1	1	0	0	1	1
30+ Days, # Rate	0%	0%	0%	10%	0%	10%	10%	10%	0%	0%	10%	10%

Some might rightfully point out that accounts such as account 1002 demonstrate higher risk as compared to other accounts that never go into delinquency. If we want to capture this information, there is an Ever Delinquency Rate to use.

Ever Delinquency Rate

Using the same example of 10-account origination vintage, Exhibit 6-8 captures all the accounts that are currently 30+ days delinquent or that were ever 30+ days delinquent. The difference from the Spot Delinquency Rate calculation is that, with the example of account 1002, even though its status becomes current in September and forward, it is still counted as 30+ days "ever" delinquent.

Exhibit 6-8 Ever Delinquency Rate

Account ID	Jan '20	Feb	Mar	Apr	May	Jun	Jul	Aug	Sep	Oct	Nov	Dec
1001												
1002						1	1	1	1	1	1	1
1003												
1004												
1005				1	1	1	1	1	1	1	1	1
1006												
1007												
1008											1	1
1009												
1010												
Total # Ever 30+	0	0	0	1	1	2	2	2	2	2	3	3
Ever 30+ Days, # Rate	0%	0%	0%	10%	10%	20%	20%	20%	20%	20%	30%	30%

The ever delinquency rate is often used when the occurrence of delinquency accounts is relatively rare compared to the size of the origination vintage. By using the ever delinquency rate, it is easier to spot the risk trend of a vintage early on.

Exhibit 6-9 shows the same Spot 30+ days delinquency rate and Ever 30+ days delinquency rate as side-by-side curves.

This illustrates that, for a given origination vintage, the Spot delinquency curve could fluctuate as accounts go in and out of delinquency buckets. However, the Ever delinquency curve never goes down, as it always counts previously delinquent accounts.

Exhibit 6-9   Spot Delinquency Curve vs. Ever Delinquency Curve

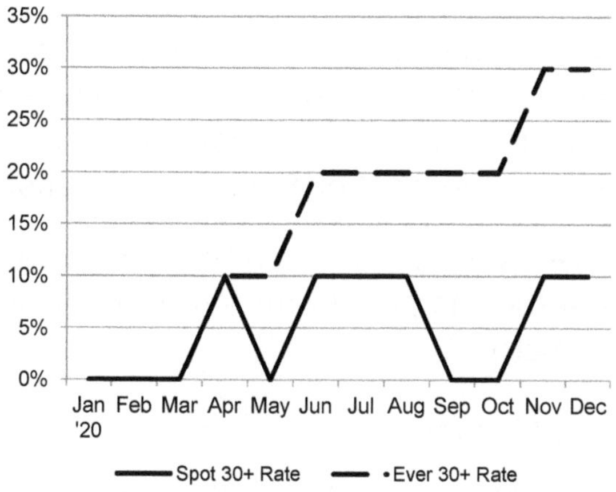

Unit Rate and Dollar Rate

The examples above use the number of accounts to calculate the delinquency rate, which is often referred to as "unit rate" or "incidence rate." Another similar metric is to use the balance of accounts to calculate the delinquency rate, which is then referred as the "dollar rate." Both metrics are commonly used, but some would put more emphasis on a dollar rate as it is more indicative of the final dollar loss rate and loss amount.

30+, 60+, and 90+ Days Delinquency Rate

Besides the 30+ days delinquency ratios used in the previous examples, lenders often also use 60+ days and 90+ days to measure the risk of vintages.

The 30+ days delinquency ratio allows a lender to observe the trend of delinquency early on, such as accounts being 6 months on book. As the vintage becomes more seasoned, 60+ or 90+ days delinquency ratios can be introduced.

Vintage Charge-off Curves

Once a credit account is opened, the first payment due date is usually one month later. In the case of a revolving credit product, some account holders might not use the revolving account right away, so the real due date of the first payment may arrive even later.

If we suppose a typical charge-off policy under which accounts that are delinquent 180 days or more should be classified as charge-off (officially recognized as a loss), the charge-off usually starts to emerge in month 7 or 8 for an origination vintage.

Thus, for vintages with 12 month-on-book and beyond, it makes sense to look at the charge-off rate, which probably is the most important risk metric.

Unit Charge-off Rate

Similar to delinquency rates, there are the unit/incidence loss rate and the dollar loss rate.

The unit charge-off rate is equal to the number of charge-offs divided by the total number of accounts in the vintage.

Dollar Charge-off Rate

For a revolving product like the credit card, it is a bit challenging to link the final charge-off balance to the initial purchase transactions, as accounts could carry a balance from month to month, which is called "revolving."

One way to calculate the dollar charge-off rate is to use the total amount of charge-offs in the last 12 months divided by the average balance in the last 12 months. Conceptually, this supposes that loss comes from the balance over the last 12-month period.

For a vintage that has not reached 12 month-on-book yet, let's use month-on-book at 6 as an example. The calculation just becomes the total amount of charge-offs in the first 6 months divided by the average balance in the first 6 months.

Once the vintage reaches 7 months-on-book, the calculation of dollar charge-off rate then becomes the total amount of charge-offs in the first 7 months divided by the average balance in the first 7 months, etc. An example of such a calculation for a credit card vintage is shown in Exhibit 6-10.

Exhibit 6-10 Dollar Charge-off Rate for Credit Card Vintage

MOB	1	2	3	4	5	6	7	8	9	10	11	12
Balance ($000)	$ 5.0	$ 11.0	$ 13.0	$ 15.0	$ 19.0	$ 20.0	$ 22.0	$ 27.0	$ 28.0	$ 30.0	$ 35.0	$ 36.0
Avg Bal(1-n)	$ 5.0	$ 8.0	$ 9.0	$ 10.0	$ 12.0	$ 12.5	$ 13.5	$ 16.0	$ 16.5	$ 17.5	$ 20.0	$ 20.5
Charge-off ($000)	$ -	$ -	$ -	$ -	$ -	$ 0.1	$ 0.6	$ 1.3	$ 1.6	$ 1.4	$ 1.3	$ 1.1
$ CO Rate	0.00%	0.00%	0.00%	0.00%	0.00%	0.80%	4.44%	8.13%	9.70%	8.00%	6.50%	5.37%

For installment loans, the dollar charge-off rate can be calculated the same way as above, or simply against the original loan amount.

An increase of delinquency will lead to an increase of charge-off. Thus, it is important to monitor the trend of the delinquencies.

Paydown / Payoff Curve

Another important measurement of installment loan vintage is the paydown curve, which shows how fast customers pay down the initial loan amount.

Exhibit 6-11 shows the paydown curves of recent quarterly vintages from an installment loan portfolio. The rate at each observation point is simply the outstanding percentage balance relative to the initial loan amount at a given month-on-book.

You can see that the more recent vintage experiences a slower paydown rate, which indicates a potential deterioration of credit. This should be looked into further, with other measurements such as delinquency curves and loan composition.

Exhibit 6-11 Paydown Curves of Installment Loan Vintages

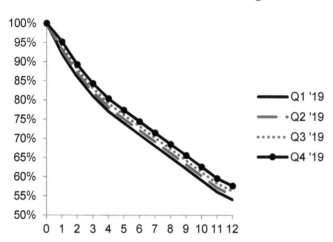

In practice, some might prefer to invert the paydown curves to show pay-off curves instead. Each data point simply becomes the cumulative paid off balance divided by the original loan amount.

6.3 Champion/Challenger Design

All the measurements mentioned above can also be used to compare strategies in a champion/challenger setting.

Champion/challenger design is actually widely used across all decision areas. The idea is to run a new strategy, the challenger, along with the incumbent strategy, the champion, side by side.

In order to isolate any other factors, the assignment of champion vs. challenger strategies is driven by a random number generated for each application. Let's say it is a 2-digit random number in the range of 00–99.

For the rollout of a challenger strategy, we want to be cautious, so we have decided to assign it only to 20% of the overall application universe. This can be achieved by assigning a random number between 00 and 19 to the challenger. The remaining 80% with a random number between 20 and 99 is still assigned with the incumbent champion strategy.

Because of the random strategy assignment, any difference in performance between the random number groups 00–19 and 20–99 can be attributed to the difference between the two strategies.

Next, let's look at an example of how a lender evaluates a challenger origination strategy.

Example 6-1 A Promising New Origination Challenger Strategy

A lender implemented a new origination challenger strategy last year. Now there is 12-month performance available for the first quarterly origination vintage.

Exhibit 6-12 shows that the approval rate of the challenger on average is 250 bps higher than that of the champion, while the $90+ delinquency rate and the $ charge-off rates under the two strategies are similar.

Exhibit 6-12 12-month Performance of First Quarterly Vintage

Strategy	Random Digit	# Applications	# Approved	Approval %	12M $ 90+ Rate	12M $ CO Rate
Challenger	00 - 19	2,000	1,250	62.5%	3.50%	8.12%
Champion	20 - 99	8,000	4,800	60.0%	3.55%	8.10%

The performance of the challenger strategy was also close to the original expectation. It is promising to become the new champion.

The lender decided to continue to monitor the performance for another 3 months before making any decision on the challenger strategy. At that time, the second quarterly vintage will have 12 months of performance and the first quarterly vintage will have 15 months of performance.

Please note that the degree of difference in performance can drive the decision of the challenger strategy earlier in the vintage analysis. In the example above, another option for the lender is to increase the assignment of the challenger strategy from 20% to 40%, given its favorable performance in approval rate and comparable $ charge-off rate.

If all performance metrics still look good for the challenger strategy 3 months later, the lender can claim it as the new champion and assign it to 100% of the application population.

Once new accounts become more seasoned, they will be subject to more credit decisions. Let's move further along the credit life cycle to look at account management decision areas.

For installment loans, once accounts are approved and funds are provided, the only risk mitigating controls are collection related strategies. For revolving products such as credit cards and lines of credit, there are more levers available such as authorizations and credit line management, which will be examined in detail in the next section.

SECTION III
ACCOUNT MANAGEMENT

Chapter 7
Authorization

When a credit card is swiped or keyed in for a purchase, an authorization transaction will be sent to the card issuer to see if there is enough credit available and whether it would pass all the risk and fraud checks. In the end, a decision will be returned either as an approval or as a decline. This process is called authorization.

Authorization applies to lines of credit as well, just typically with a less advanced strategy. This chapter will use credit card to illustrate the process.

7.1   Authorization Controls

An authorization typically needs to go through a series of risk and fraud checks before finally getting approved. If the authorization fails any of the checks during the process, the decision would be a decline.

These risk and fraud checks during the authorization process can be loosely classified into three categories.

☑ Credit Policy

☑ Fraud Rules

☑ Credit Risk Authorization Strategy

Exhibit 7-1 Authorization Workflow

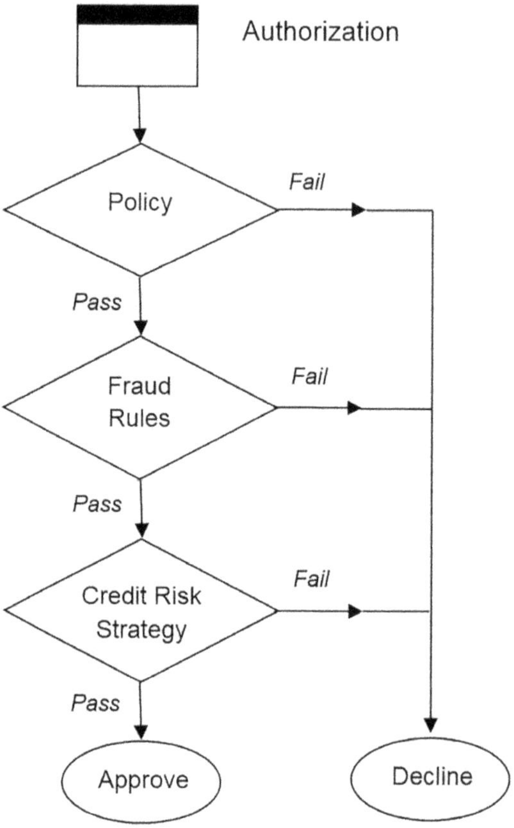

Credit Policy

For authorization, the card issuer typically has certain policies in place to deal with some common scenarios.

For example, an authorization from a credit card account that has already been closed will be declined. Similarly, authorization from an account already in bankruptcy or charge-off status will be declined as well.

How this works is that there is a rule during the authorization stream to check the status code of the account. If the status code indicates that the account is closed, bankrupt, or charged off, then the result will be a decline.

Besides an account status check, there are other credit policies such as PIN verification, card verification value (CVV) check, and expiration date check. These example controls would stop authorizations from lost/stolen cards, counterfeit cards, and expired cards.

A card issuer processor typically provides tools to implement these basic credit policies. For example, FDR (First Data Resources) allows its clients to define some of the credit policies through product control file (PCF) settings.

Fraud Rules

If a card falls into the hands of a fraudster, the best time to mitigate the risk is at the time of authorization. Once the authorization is approved, it will take a lot of effort for a lender to recover some of the loss resulting from the fraud.

If an authorization looks suspicious, the card issuer can opt to decline the authorization, thus stopping potential loss due to fraud.

One suspicious transaction scenario is excessive authorizations within a short period of time. Another scenario is that of multiple authorizations happening in different geographic areas; the geographic locations are so distant from each other that it is not possible for the cardholder to travel from one to the other with any reasonable mode of transportation. For a list of possible scenarios associated with authorization decline, please refer to Section 15.3 Transactional Fraud.

A card issuer processor usually provides the toolkit for the card issuer to implement a suite of transactional fraud strategies (also known as account management fraud strategies), which can directly decline authorizations or put them in fraud queues for manual review.

If an authorization passes both the credit policy and fraud rules, it will continue to the next key component — the credit risk authorization strategy.

Credit Risk Authorization Strategy

In the credit risk authorization strategy, the authorization transaction will be evaluated against the available open-to-buy of the account.

If the authorization amount plus the existing balance is within the credit limit, the decision will be an approval. The vast majority of authorizations follow this scenario.

However, if an authorization and existing balance would bring the account over its credit limit, it does not mean that a decline decision will be automatic. Card issuers have the option to approve the overlimit authorization if the associated risk is deemed acceptable. This is where the credit risk authorization strategy comes into play.

Similarly, for authorizations from delinquent accounts, card issuers can also use authorization strategy to make an approval or decline decision.

The idea is to provide cardholder convenience if the associated risk is deemed low — which usually is the case if a transaction would only bring the new balance over the credit limit by a few dollars or when the cardholder misses a payment due only by a few days.

Section 7.2 provides a more detailed introduction of the credit risk authorization strategy, which is what authorization strategy usually refers to in the context of credit risk management.

7.2 Authorization Strategy

Once an authorization passes credit policy and fraud rules and flows into the adaptive control system for credit risk assessment, a predefined authorization strategy will be deployed to evaluate the risk of the transaction and give an approval as opposed to a decline decision.

The decisions usually focus on overlimit authorizations and delinquent authorizations, whereas the under-the-limit authorization from current accounts typically gets immediate approval.

As with other credit risk strategies, authorization strategy is usually decision tree based, which makes it easy and intuitive to communicate with the management team and business stakeholders.

7.2.1 Decision Elements

The selection of decision elements (also known as decision keys) in a credit risk strategy can be business driven, i.e., to enable a business rule such as disallowing overlimit if the accountholder has opted out of overlimit. They can also be data driven, i.e., identified as strong risk predictors through data analysis.

Typical decision elements used in an authorization strategy include:

- ☑ Account Status Code
- ☑ Days Delinquent
- ☑ Months on Book
- ☑ Credit Limit
- ☑ Open to Buy
- ☑ Utilization
- ☑ Credit Bureau Score - the latest refreshed score
- ☑ Behavior Score
- ☑ Overlimit Opt-in/Opt-out Indicator
- ☑ Recent Payment Behavior — for example:
  - ‣ Payment/balance Ratio in the last 3 months
  - ‣ Payment/limit Ratio in the last 6 months
  - ‣ Number of Returned Payments
  - ‣ Days since Last Returned Payment

☑ Account Activity related
  ‣ Number of months inactive
  ‣ Number of months active

☑ Authorization Amount

☑ POS Entry Mode — such as swipe, key in, e-commerce

☑ Merchant Category Code (MCC)

A full-service bank can also leverage the information of other banking relationships the accountholder has with the same bank, which often provides additional risk separation power.

Examples of relationship-based decision elements include:

☑ Presence of Primary Banking Relationship

  ‣ Presence of mortgage

  ‣ Presence of deposit account with active debit/credit transactions

☑ Tenure of Banking Relationship

☑ Balance in the deposit accounts - such as the average deposit account balance in the last 6 months

☑ Overdraft history with deposit accounts - such as the average overdraft balance in the last 3 months

☑ Non-Sufficient Fund (NSF) history with deposit accounts — such as the number of NSFs that have occurred in the last 6 months

The examples mentioned above could be used in other decision strategies as well. To avoid repetition, they will be referred to as "banking relationship" decision elements going forward.

7.2.2   Action

The action of an authorization is usually simply a decline or approval decision. With approval, the issuer can also decide the dollar amount allowed above the existing credit limit, which is called an overlimit pad or an overlimit cushion. This pad or cushion can also be defined as a percentage of the existing credit limit.

Actions for Overlimit Authorization

The overlimit cushion assigned to overlimit authorization is usually within 25% of the existing limit. If an authorization is determined to be low risk, the cushion assigned would tend toward the higher end. Relatively higher risk will be assigned a cushion toward the lower end. The high risk authorizations beyond the portfolio's risk appetite will simply not get any cushion.

Exhibit 7-2 shows a set of actions for current accounts, with the overlimit cushion assigned based on the expected dollar loss rate.

Exhibit 7-2   Sample Actions for Current Accounts

$ Loss Rate	<= $10K	> $10K
<= 1.00%	125%	$2,500
1.01% - 2.00%	120%	$2,250
2.01% - 3.00%	115%	115%
3.01% - 4.00%	110%	110%
4.01% - 6.00%	105%	105%
6.01% - 8.00%	$100	$200
8.01+%	$0	$0

Actions for Delinquent Merchandise Authorization

As some customers tend to forget their credit card payment due dates and often pay a few days late, or did not open the credit card bill due to an extended vacation, an authorization from such delinquent accounts usually carries low credit risk. In these cases, it makes sense for the issuer to approve such authorizations selectively.

Actually, issuers often approve small authorizations even though the account is 15 to 20 days delinquent.

However, once an account is more than 5 days delinquent, issuers typically cap the maximum allowed authorization plus existing balance only to a portion of the credit limit.

For example, an account is 10 days delinquent, with a decent credit bureau score of 720 and a behavior score of 685. Upon analysis, the risk of accounts with such a credit profile has a 12-month expected dollar loss rate of 1.5%. Based on Exhibit 7-3, the action assigned will be an approval of up to 70% of the existing credit limit.

Exhibit 7-3 Sample Actions for Delinquent Accounts

$ Loss Rate	Days Delinquent		
	1-5 Days	6-15 Days	16+ Days
<= 1.00%	100%	75%	Decline
1.01% - 2.00%	95%	70%	Decline
2.01% - 3.00%	90%	65%	Decline
3.01% - 4.00%	85%	60%	Decline
4.01% - 6.00%	80%	55%	Decline
6.01% - 8.00%	75%	50%	Decline
8.01+%	Decline	Decline	Decline

Action for Cash Authorizations

Action for cash authorizations is relatively straightforward.

As access to cash via credit card is only meant to be used in case of emergency or out of convenience, there should not be any overlimit cash authorization allowed beyond the cash line.

For current accounts with low risk scores, the cash access can be further limited to a percentage of the cash line. You might want to check with your legal and compliance colleagues to discuss how tight your cash authorization for current accounts should be in order to comply with local laws and regulations.

For a delinquent account, the cash access should be forfeited altogether, i.e., no cash access allowed.

Exhibit 7-4 shows a set of actions for cash authorizations, also based on assessed risk levels.

Exhibit 7-4 Sample Actions for Cash Authorizations

$ Loss Rate	Current	Delinquent
<= 8.00%	100%	Decline
8.01% - 10.00%	75%	Decline
10.01% - 15.00%	50%	Decline
15.01+%	Decline	Decline

7.2.3 A Sample Authorization Strategy

Exhibit 7-5 shows a simplified authorization strategy. For the sake of clarity, the strategy only applies to regular merchandise authorizations, which comprise the vast majority of the authorizations anyway.

The first decision element is Days Delinquent. As most accounts are current, the vast majority of authorizations will flow to the left branch where Days Delinquent <= 0.

Exhibit 7-5 A Sample Authorization Strategy

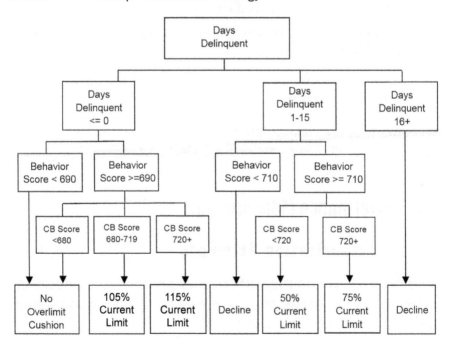

Based on their behavior score and credit bureau score (CB Score), these current accounts are segmented further into nodes with different risk levels.

☑ The low risk node (high scores) is assigned an overlimit cushion of 15% of the account's credit limit.

☑ The high risk nodes (low scores) do not have overlimit cushion assigned — that means those accounts are not allowed to go overlimit.

☑ The medium risk node is assigned a 5% overlimit cushion.

Accounts that are only 1–15 days delinquent go down the middle branch of Days Delinquent 1–15. As some customers could simply have forgotten the payment due date or it could take a few days for customer-initiated payments to post on the account, the low risk authorizations from this segment can still be allowed to transact.

☑ The low risk node (high scores) is allowed to transact up to 75% of the account's credit limit.

☑ The medium risk node is allowed to transact up to 50% of the account's credit limit.

☑ The high risk node (low scores) is not allowed to have any authorization go through — they are declined.

Accounts that are delinquent 16 days or more are deemed high risk and thus all authorizations are declined.

7.3 Performance Measurement

7.3.1 Authorization Attempts

To understand where the authorizations requiring risk decisions come in, it is necessary to measure these authorization attempts using multiple dimensions.

Exhibit 7-6 shows the measurement of dollar overlimit authorization attempts by new utilization (if the overlimit authorization is approved).

The exhibit shows that most of the overlimit attempts should be able to be served with an overlimit cushion of up to 120% of the existing limit, if the risk level is within risk appetite.

What should be noted is that the segment with authorization attempt 131%+ also has some volumes. You might want to look at this segment further to see if there is a credit line increase opportunity, as this range is typically beyond the reach of overlimit authorization strategy.

Exhibit 7-6 $ Overlimit Attempt by New Utilization ($ Million)

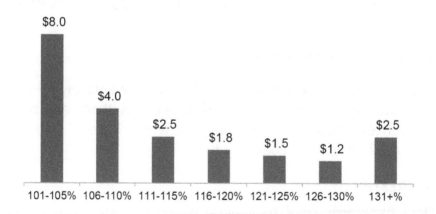

Assume that you have decided to focus on the overlimit authorizations within 125% of the existing limit. You can then add another dimension by looking at the existing credit limit.

Once you chart the overlimit authorization distribution by new utilization and the existing credit limit, as in Exhibit 7-7, it is easy to see that most of the dollar approval opportunities are within the Limit <= $15K segments.

Exhibit 7-7 $ Overlimit Attempt by New Utilization and Current Limit

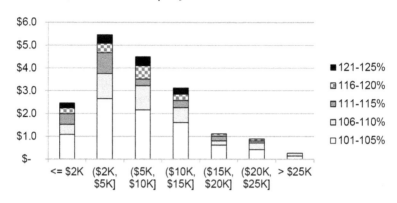

Knowing where the opportunity is, you can analyze further to see what appropriate actions can be taken in those segments to boost authorization approval rate with an acceptable risk level.

7.3.2 Approval Rate

Approval rate is a key metric that is monitored closely by both business and risk teams at card issuers. As there are some differences between a bankcard and a retail credit card and they are introduced separately here.

Bankcard

Here bankcards refer to general purpose credit cards issued by banks or credit unions. They can be used anywhere their associated card networks reach.

From a business perspective, the authorization approval rate has a direct impact on purchase, interchange fee, account balance, and customer experience, and is thus a very important metric.

Bankcards usually have a unit authorization approval rate of around 95%–96%. The dollar authorization approval rate is slightly lower, as declined transactions tend to have large transaction amounts.

Card issuers always look for opportunities to increase their authorization approval rates in order to grow sales and balances. One way to evaluate potential opportunity is to examine authorization attempts by risk score.

Profile by Credit Bureau Score

Exhibit 7-8 shows an example of the dollar approval rate of overlimit authorizations by credit bureau score. It also combines the distribution of dollar overlimit authorization attempts.

Exhibit 7-8 $ Overlimit Attempts ($ Millions) and $ Approval Rate by FICO

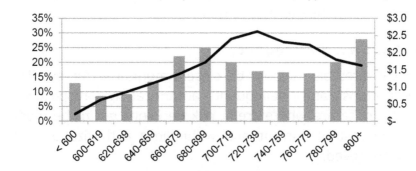

$ Auth Attempt, $M (Right)　　$ Approval Rate (Left)

The exhibit shows that the low risk segments, especially a credit bureau score of 780+, currently have lower dollar approval rates, which also have sizable authorization attempts. This indicates that there are probably some opportunities to increase the dollar approval rate. Further analysis can be conducted on accounts with a credit bureau score of 780+.

A similar analysis can also be conducted on behavior score.

Domestic vs. International

Besides risk score, approval rate can also be broken down into domestic vs. international authorizations. Due to fraud, the approval rate of domestic authorizations is typically higher than that of international authorizations.

Card Present vs. Card Not Present

By the way authorizations are entered at the point-of-sale (POS), authorizations can be divided into card present vs. card not present. Due to the higher fraud risk, the approval rate of card not present authorizations is lower than that of card present authorizations.

Merchandise, Cash, or Balance Transfer

Depending on the category of purchases, authorizations can be divided into merchandise, cash or balance transfer, with the approval rate of merchandise authorizations being of the greatest importance to a card issuer.

Overlimit vs. Delinquent

Approval rates also should be closely monitored for overlimit authorizations and delinquent authorizations respectively, because these are where credit risk decisions get to be made, while the rest of current and within-limit authorizations are simply approved.

According to FICO, the dollar approval rate on overlimit authorizations is around 30%–33%. The dollar approval rate on delinquent authorizations is around 60%-65%[1]. If your approval rates are below the benchmark range, you probably want to drill down further to see where the improvement opportunity is.

Retail Card

Retail cards are credit cards issued by a retailer's finance division or by a bank under a partnership with the retailer. They can only be used in the retailer's stores.

Compared to bankcards, retail cards generally have higher approval rates and lower decline rates, for the following reasons:

- ☑ A retail card portfolio tends to have a higher risk appetite, with the interest rate on the card and the margin higher than those of bankcards. Thus, it makes sense for authorizations with higher risk to be approved on retail cards, but not on bankcards.

☑ The approval rate at POS or in store is so important to the retailers. If the card program is under a partnership formed by the retailer and a bank partner, the approval rate is often written down as an important clause in the service level agreement (SLA). A higher approval rate means higher retail sales and a better customer experience.

☑ Retail card authorizations can be referred to the call center for further assessment. The higher margin of the retail card and the importance of the approval rate justify additional staff to evaluate the referred transactions. Upon assessment, some of the referred transactions will be approved.

7.3.3 Risk Measurement

There are two ways to measure the risk associated with authorizations: authorization-based and account-based. We will use examples to illustrate the difference of these two methods. As you will see, these two methods are actually not too dissimilar.

Authorization-based Method

Let's assume that we want to measure the loss performance of authorizations in a 12-month performance window.

The unit loss rate is simply:

# of authorizations on accounts becoming charge-offs in the following 12 months / Total # of authorizations approved in the observation period

The dollar loss rate is:

$ of authorizations on accounts becoming charge-offs in the following 12 months / Total $ of authorizations approved in the observation period

Account-based Method

The account-based method is intended to capture all the loss amount and balance on the accounts associated with the authorization, even though some balances are booked before or after the authorization occurs.

Under the account-based method, the unit loss rate is:

# of accounts with approved authorizations becoming charge-offs in the following 12 months / Total # of accounts with approved authorizations in the observation period

The dollar loss rate is:

Total $ balance of accounts with approved authorizations becoming charge-offs in the following 12 months / Average total $ balance of accounts with approved authorizations in the observation period

The example below illustrates the differences between these two methods of measurement.

Example 7-1 Authorization-based vs. Account-based Risk Measurement

Suppose there are 10 non-delinquent accounts with overlimit authorizations going through the authorization strategy. For the sake of simplicity, assume they all have the same credit limit of $1,000 and the same balance of $900 each when the authorizations occur.

Now, each of the 10 accounts now transacts a $200 authorization at the same time. Suppose all accounts have reasonable risk levels, thus all authorizations get approved. Then each account becomes 10% overlimit with $1,100 new balance ($900 existing balance + $200 approved authorization) vs. $1,000 existing credit limit.

Twelve months later, only 1 out of the 10 accounts becomes a charge-off and the other 9 accounts are still current and in good standing. The charge-off account has a loss amount of $1,100. Again, for simplicity's sake, assume the average balance in the 12-month performance period for each account is $1,000.

Now let's calculate the loss rates under two different measurement methods.

Under the Authorization-based Method

Unit loss rate: 1 authorization from the charge-off account / all 10 authorizations = 10%

Dollar loss rate: the $200 authorization associated with the charge-off account / $2,000 total approved authorization amount (10 * $200 each) = 10%

Under the Account-based Method

Unit loss rate: 1 account that becomes a charge-off / 10 accounts = 10%

Dollar loss rate: the $1,100 charge-off amount from the charge-off account / the average total balance of 10 accounts in 12 months = $1,100 / (10 * $1,000) = $1,100 / $10,000 = 11%.

In the example above, the unit loss rates are the same using either the authorization-based method or the account-based method.

The dollar loss rate under the account-based method is 11%, slightly higher than the 10% under the authorization-based approach. This is due to the fact that the charge-off amount of the bad account, $1,100, is higher than the average account balance of the good accounts, $1,000, while the authorizations on both the charged-off account and the good accounts are all the same at $200.

One takeaway from the example above is that the unit and dollar loss rates under both methods are not too far away from each other, as the performances reflect the behaviors from the same group of accounts.

If there are stakeholders who have different preferences, you can always provide both types of measurement.

Performance Period

The performance period used in the example above is 12 months, which is a typical time frame in which to review various credit risk strategies. However, this performance period is not set in stone. Actually, people often want to have an early read of the strategy's performance.

For authorization approval rate, this will be available right away in the first month when a new authorization strategy is implemented. However, for risk performance, the performance has to wait a bit longer.

After 6 months, most of the loss has probably not occurred yet, but the delinquency begins to emerge. The risk measurement can be adjusted to a 30+ day delinquency rate, including charge-offs.

After 9 months, as some high risk accounts move into late stage delinquency, the risk measurement can be changed to a 90+ day delinquency rate, including charge-offs.

In summary, you can always adjust the definition of "bad," based on the length of the performance period in order to have meaningful measurements.

7.4   Incorporation of Fraud Strategy

In practice, some card issuers might decide to incorporate fraud mitigation strategy into the credit risk authorization strategy so that a suspicious transaction can be declined in real-time and the account in question can be blocked.

While the additional controls would definitely help those card issuers mitigate fraud losses, it does complicate the credit risk authorization strategy, which now serves dual functions as both risk strategy and fraud strategy.

This would lead to more frequent changes in authorization strategies, which increases the chance of mistakes in implementation. With authorization strategy and fraud strategy intertwined, another risk is that a particular change in one area might unintentionally generate negative impacts in the other area.

Therefore, if a card issuer does decide to incorporate fraud strategy into authorization strategy, enough resources on the implementation side need to be assigned and well trained so that the comprehensive authorization and fraud strategies can be understood and coded correctly.

Thorough testing is always desirable in order to catch any defect before a new strategy is released into the production environment. Because the results of authorization decisions are immediately visible to cardholders, any defect, especially an erroneous decline, will create a bad customer experience, lead to customer complaints, and cause customers to abandon their cards.

Chapter 8
Credit Line Increase

As a revolving credit account matures, a lender might notice that some customers deserve a credit line increase so their growing credit needs can be better accommodated.

Depending on whether the credit line increase is initiated by the customer or the lender, as well as how the offer is delivered to the customer per a particular jurisdiction's regulation, a lender can deploy different credit line increase programs. Sections 8.1–8.4 provide an introduction to each of the different programs. Sections 8.5–8.6 present the composition of a credit increase strategy and the performance measurement.

8.1 Reactive Credit Line Increase

A typical scenario is that the customer reaches out to the lender to request a credit line increase (CLI), which is a clear indication that the current credit line is insufficient to satisfy the customer's current or near-term credit need.

As a customer's CLI request is usually evaluated right away, this is also referred as "Online CLI".

Call in

A call center is a main channel for receiving the credit line increase request. If a customer submits the CLI request via phone, the agent who answers the call can trigger a reactive credit line increase strategy to evaluate the request after asking a few questions. The decision will be returned instantly and the agent can then tell the customer the result over the phone.

Internet

Besides a phone call, a customer can also submit the CLI request online, which can usually be found as a menu option when the customer logs into the online account. Similarly, the request will be routed to the same reactive credit line increase strategy for review. The decision will be returned instantly online to the customer.

Request Credit Line

When requesting a CLI, a customer can request a specific new credit line amount, such as $5,000. This request credit line will go into the strategy for consideration.

If the customer qualifies for a new credit line of $5,000 or more, the requested $5,000 will be granted. If the customer only qualifies for a lower line (but still higher than the existing credit line), let's say $4,000, then only $4,000 will be presented to the customer.

8.2 Proactive Credit Line Increase

Reactive CLI only accounts for a small percentage of the actual line increase. Most line increases are handed out proactively by lenders.

This is because lenders have access to the behavior histories and credit bureau attributes of their own customers, which allows the lenders to make a fairly good assessment in terms of who is qualified for a credit line increase.

Pre-2009

Before the Great Recession from 2008 to 2010, card issuers could pretty much hand out CLIs freely, as long as the accounts were deemed creditworthy. This was the case in both the U.S. and Canada.

However, after the financial crisis, the regulators on both sides of the border introduced their own legislation to add additional requirements regarding the Proactive CLI, which has effectively slowed down credit extensions under this tactic for credit cards[1].

The U.S. CARD Act

In the U.S., the CARD Act was enacted as part of the broad Dodd-Frank Act, which requires credit card issuers to evaluate a borrower's ability to pay at the time of origination and extending credit line increase[2].

Under the ability-to-pay clause, a lender has to use one of the following three ways to evaluate a borrower's repayment capability:

☑ Debt-to-income ratio

☑ Debt-to-asset ratio

☑ Residual income

The debt-to-income ratio is the method most widely used, sometimes in combination with the other two methods. As mentioned in Chapter 4, "Origination Channel," lenders can access a borrower's credit bureau file to obtain the debt information. However, the up-to-date income data still needs to be collected. Next, we will look at a few typical ways to collect income data.

Income

Consumers do provide their income at the time of origination, but the income at origination only has a limited shelf life. Generally, the income information that is less than 12 months old is still considered good to use.

For accounts on the books more than 12 months, lenders typically use the following ways to get up-to-date income information:

☑ Ask the customer directly — via mail, email, online message, etc.

☑ Estimate the income based on cash inflow from a deposit account — for full-service banks only.

☑ Purchase verified income — Equifax provides such a service via its The Work Number solution.

☑ Use Income Estimator, which provides estimated income based on a statistical model — provided by major credit bureaus.

No matter which way(s) a lender adopts, it is important that the lender follows a prudent test-and-learn approach and make sure the CLIs are granted to customers who are creditworthy and responsive to the CLI.

The effects of a CLI strategy should be monitored closely and be well documented, which is essential to meet internal portfolio management's need, as well as regulatory requirements.

Canada

Before the 2008 Financial Crisis, Canada adopted the traditional Proactive CLI model for most of its provinces and territories, except the Province of Quebec. After the crisis, Canada switched to a customer consent model, which was what the Province of Quebec had been using all along. This will be explained in detail in Section 8.4.

8.3 Pre-select Credit Line Increase

With the ability-to-pay requirement, there is a good portion of credit card accounts that do not have the latest income available. The reason could be that the cardholders do not want to share recent income out of concern over their privacy or the card issuer does not have the budget to purchase verified income information. Whatever the reason, the card issuer cannot proactively extend the CLI without the updated income.

One way to extract the potential CLI needs is via a pre-select CLI campaign.

Since a card issuer has access to all internal data and credit bureau attributes of its accounts, it can run the whole CLI credit risk strategy against the portfolio — except the ability-to-pay rule — and produce a list of CLI eligible accounts.

Then, communication via direct mail or email can be sent to this pre-selected list of customers, advising that they are prequalified for CLI and can contact the card issuer to apply for one.

This pre-selection approach is still a well-targeted method to best utilize the budget. However, because a portion of the subsequent CLI requests will inevitably be declined due to the ability-to-pay rule, the wording of the solicitation materials should be carefully drafted and avoid offering the false impression that the CLI is guaranteed.

8.4 Preapproved Credit Line Increase

One approach that is similar to the pre-select approach, but provides more certainty for the customer, is the preapproved CLI approach. This was widely adopted in Canada after the 2008 financial crisis.

In September 2009, with the objective of increasing protection of consumers of financial products, the Government of Canada passed the Credit Business Practices Regulations. One of the regulations stipulates that financial institutions need to obtain express consents from consumers before increasing the credit limits of their credit cards[3].

This practice actually was already in place in Quebec, the French-speaking province in Canada. Quebec has its own legislatures which is often pro-consumer.

Under the new regulation, although lenders cannot increase the credit line of consumer cards automatically, they still possess all the information needed to evaluate which accounts are qualified for CLI.

Thus a lender can continue to run the CLI strategy on every billing cycle and produce a list of CLI-eligible accounts. Then the lender can proactively reach out to qualified customers and present the CLI offers. All the consumer needs to do is provide consent to the lender, then the CLI will take place. Thus, this is a true preapproved CLI offer. There is no additional question such as income being asked, as Canada does not have the ability-to-pay requirement.

It should be noted that even though it is called preapproved, still not 100% of responders will be granted a CLI. The exception could occur when an account's credit deteriorates after the preapproval offer is made, such as becoming delinquent.

That is why there is usually fine print in the CLI preapproval communication, stating that the offer is valid only when the account remains in good status. In practice, there is always a final check of an account's latest status when the cardholder responds to the offer.

Omnichannel

For a full-service bank with an established branch and ATM network, all channels can be leveraged to market the preapproved CLI offers to customers at each interaction opportunity.

For example, when a qualified customer walks into the branch or calls the call center, a prompt screen will pop up on the teller or customer service agent's screen, which indicates that the customer has a preapproved CLI offer for their credit card.

Once this offer is presented and accepted by the customer, the CLI goes into effect. The smooth process provides a positive experience to the consumer.

Similarly, a message can be presented when the customer logs into online banking or at an ATM machine. By clicking a button on the menu to provide consent, the CLI will be granted via the digital channel.

In addition, traditional direct mail and email can also be deployed to send out the pre-approved offer.

So far, we have learned the four major types of credit line increase programs. Next, let's look at the composition of a typical credit line increase risk strategy.

8.5 Credit Line Increase Strategy

8.5.1 Decision Elements

The typical decision elements used in a CLI strategy include:

- ☑ Account Status Code
- ☑ VIP, Insider (Regulation O), Private Banking Indicator
- ☑ Self-identified CLI Exclusion Indicator
- ☑ Time Since Last Credit Line Change — accounts with recent line change typically are excluded, such as:
    - ‣ CLI occurrence in the previous 9 or 12 months
    - ‣ CLD occurrence in the previous 12 months
- ☑ Existing Credit Line
- ☑ Balance
- ☑ Utilization
    - ‣ Current Utilization
    - ‣ Average Utilization in the previous 3 or 6 Months
- ☑ Months on Book
- ☑ Credit Bureau Score - the latest refreshed score
- ☑ Behavior Score
- ☑ Delinquency Status
- ☑ Bankruptcy Score
- ☑ Spend Level
- ☑ Competitive Credit Limit, if available from the credit bureau refresh process
- ☑ Age — depending on your local regulation on how a consumer's age can be used
- ☑ Banking Relationship — see Section 7.2.1 for details

8.5.2   Sample CLI Decision Strategy

Exhibit 8-1 shows a simple CLI decision strategy as an example. The decision tree essentially only allows accounts meeting all of the following criteria to receive a CLI:

☑   Current accounts

☑   No limit change in the last 12 months

☑   Behavior score >= 680

☑   Credit bureau score >= 660

☑   Average utilization in the last 6 months >= 30%

Exhibit 8-1   Sample CLI Decision Strategy

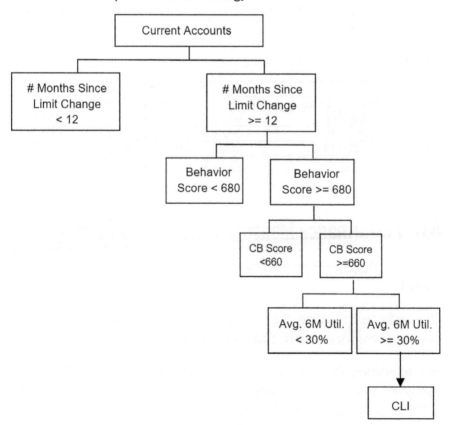

In the U.S., where an ability-to-pay requirement exists, the accounts passing the decision tree also need to go through an ability-to-pay check based on income, housing expense, and current debt. This is usually evaluated in a separate module in the decision engine.

8.5.3 CLI Actions

Once an account passes the CLI decision strategy, including the ability-to-pay rule (if it applies), it is time to assess the amount of the CLI. The amount of the CLI is typically determined based on the account's risk level.

Exhibit 8-2 shows an example of how the amount of the CLI is assigned based on the individual's credit bureau score and behavior score.

Exhibit 8–2 CLI Amount by Dual Scores

Behavior Score	Credit Bureau Score			
	660-679	680-719	720-739	740+
680-699	$ 500	$ 500	$ 1,000	$ 1,500
700-719	$ 1,000	$ 1,500	$ 2,000	$ 2,000
720-739	$ 1,500	$ 2,000	$ 2,500	$ 2,500
740+	$ 2,000	$ 2,500	$ 2,500	$ 3,000

8.6 Performance Measurement of a CLI Strategy

8.6.1 Performance Measurement at Portfolio Level

One way to measure the effect of a CLI strategy is to measure key performance metrics at the portfolio level.

For example, for the same credit card product, portfolio A is assigned with a CLI strategy, while portfolio B does not have a CLI strategy assigned. The division of portfolio A vs. B is driven by a random number, and all the other treatments these two portfolios receive are the same.

Under this setup, any difference of balance and risk between portfolio A and portfolio B can be attributed to the CLI strategy.

Although the difference in portfolio performance is driven by the actual CLIs, operationally it is easier to track the performance of *ALL* accounts in the portfolio, including both accounts with a CLI and accounts without a CLI.

This is an easy and reasonable way to measure the impact from a strategy that is run continuously over multiple months and years.

When a CLI strategy is automatically run in the decision engine, some accounts that do not qualify in one month might qualify in the following month. Some accounts might receive the CLI again twelve months after the first CLI.

With the CLI strategy being run continuously, every month, operationally it becomes more complicated to track the accounts receiving actual CLIs vs. their corresponding control group every month. Portfolio level tracking would save all the work.

Example 8-1 A Winning CLI Challenger Strategy

In this example, we are looking at the performance of CLI strategies on a credit card portfolio with 1 million accounts.

Among the 1 million accounts, 10% are assigned with a challenger CLI strategy that was introduced 24 months prior. The other 90% are assigned with a champion strategy that has been running for years. The assignment is achieved via a random digit and the 10% and 90% portfolios do not receive differential treatments in other decision areas.

During the 24 months, there are some accounts who receive a CLI only once and some others who receive a CLI twice. There are some accounts who receive a CLI early on in month 1 and others who receive the CLI fairly late in month 18.

Regardless of all the details of the frequency and timing of actual CLIs, the performance tracking can simply be based on the overall impact on 100,000 accounts vs. 900,000 accounts. This approach presents the impact at portfolio level and makes the tracking relatively easy.

Exhibit 8-3 shows that the average balance per account under the CLI challenger strategy grew slightly after it was introduced. Then the average balance became stabilized after about 12 months. In this example, the incremental balance under the challenger strategy was expected, as it provides more generous CLI amounts and only targets those who are most likely to use the increased credit room.

Exhibit 8-3 Average Balance – CLI Champion vs. Challenger

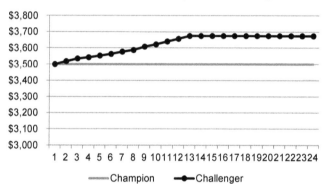

In Exhibit 8-4, the challenger strategy actually has a slightly lower loss rate. This is because the challenger strategy is still very disciplined and targets only those with acceptable risk. In addition, the effect of an increasing balance lowers the loss rate slightly.

Exhibit 8-4 $ Loss Rate – CLI Champion vs. Challenger

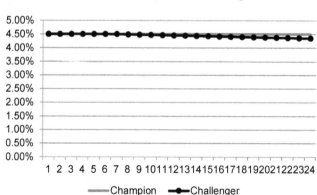

With an increasing balance and a similar loss rate, the CLI challenger is qualified to become the new champion strategy.

8.6.2 Performance Measurement at Campaign Level

If a CLI program is only run occasionally as a campaign, such as once a year, the tracking will just focus on accounts associated with each campaign.

Under the campaign level tracking, the metrics are typically based on accounts that actually receive CLIs. It is important to have a control group, which are accounts that were qualified for a CLI but were kept outside of the campaign targets. The purpose of a control group is to maintain a baseline scenario where no CLI is performed.

To better illustrate the performance measurement at campaign level, we will next look at two examples. Example 8-2 presents a proactive CLI campaign while Example 8-3 uses a preselected CLI campaign.

Example 8-2 Tracking of a Proactive CLI Campaign

A lender in the U.S. has a credit card portfolio of 1 million accounts. The lender recently purchased its cardholders' verified income from a major credit bureau. With the new data element, the lender was able to run its full CLI strategy against the entire portfolio and identified 50,000 accounts eligible for CLI.

The lender kept out a randomly selected 10% or 5,000 accounts as the control group and proactively increased the credit lines on the 90%, or 45,000 accounts.

In the following months, the lender simply tracked the performance of 45,000 accounts that actually received a CLI versus the 5,000 accounts that were qualified but did not receive a CLI. As the target and control groups are randomly selected, any performance difference could be attributed to the CLI campaign itself.

Should the reactive CLI be excluded?

Among the 5,000 control accounts, there would be some that actually called in to request a CLI during the performance period. Because such a volume is small, you can simply leave these CLI accounts in the performance data. That is what actually happened in the absence of a proactive CLI campaign.

Example 8-3 Tracking a Pre-select CLI Campaign

We will use an example similar to Example 8-2, but with a little twist. The lender did not find sufficient budget to purchase verified income this year. So, it resorted to a pre-select CLI campaign.

The lender ran the CLI strategy without the ability-to-pay component against its 1 million accounts and identified 50,000 accounts that would qualify for a CLI if they all passed the debt-to-income ratio check.

The lender put 5,000 qualified accounts aside as the control group and sent direct mails to the rest of the 45,000 qualified accounts. The direct mail notified the cardholders that they are potentially qualified for a CLI. The customers were invited to call the lender's call center to apply for a CLI.

In this pre-select CLI campaign, the impact in the target group is from accounts that actually responded to the solicitation offer, passed the ability-to-pay check, and eventually received CLIs.

Post campaign analysis shows that 5% of the 45,000 target accounts actually responded by requesting a CLI; 70% of those respondents passed the ability-to-pay check and received CLIs.

Thus, the actual number of CLIs in the target group is:

*45,000 * 5% * 70% = 1,575.*

The "official" control group is the 5,000 accounts that were kept out of the 50,000 CLI-eligible accounts. However, it is not a 100% clean control group, as some accounts among the 5,000 would not qualify for CLI due to not having enough income relative to debt.

There are actually two other groups under the campaign that should also be monitored as "quasi" control groups.

Exhibit 8-5   Various Groups in a Pre-select CLI Campaign

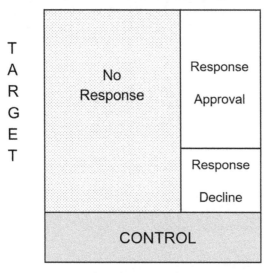

One group is the 30% who did respond to the CLI solicitation but failed the ability-to-pay requirement. They are the "Response Decline" segment in Exhibit 8-5.

The volume of the "Response Decline" population is:

*45,000 * 5% * 30% = 675 accounts.*

The other quasi control group is the non-responders among the 45,000 CLI target accounts. They are the "No Response" segment in Exhibit 8-5.

The volume of the "No Response" population is:

*45,000 * 95% = 42,750 accounts.*

The volumes of all four groups are summarized in Exhibit 8-6. Analyzing the performance of all four groups serves to better understand the customer behaviors under a pre-select CLI campaign.

Exhibit 8-6 Volume of Various Groups in a Pre-select CLI Campaign

Group		Volume
	Response - Approved	1,575
TARGET	Response - Declined	675
	No Reponse	42,750
CONTROL		5,000

Chapter 9
Credit Line Decrease

For revolving accounts, lenders frequently evaluate the risk levels of individual accounts. If the risk level of an account is deemed too high, the lender could reduce its credit line or even shut the account down to avoid future loss.

The strategy for managing the credit line decrease (CLD) and account closure due to high-risk is generally referred to as the CLD strategy.

CLD strategy is typically implemented with the same credit line management strategy as CLI strategy. However, the business scenarios that the two strategies address are very different and drive different risk criteria and notification letters. That is why they are addressed separately in two chapters.

9.1 Credit Line Decrease

When an account cycles each month, it will go through a decision tree-based credit line management strategy in the account management decision engine. If the credit risk is deemed high according to the CLD strategy's assessment, a line decrease or account closure action will be triggered and a notification letter will be sent.

9.1.1 Balance of Risk Mitigation and Customer Retention

The typical CLD targets are high-risk segments that lose money for the lenders at an aggregated level. A profitability analysis usually takes place in order to determine which segments meet such criteria.

One important aspect in the CLD strategy is that some accounts subject to the negative actions are actually good accounts, as it is impossible to separate bad accounts from good ones completely, like separating black from white, in advance.

Naturally, the good accounts that receive the CLDs would not like the decision. This negative action will cause some to quickly attrite by paying off the balance and moving their business elsewhere.

Other good accounts will now be constrained by the lower credit limits and the limited growth in balances will reduce potential income. If the lost revenue is greater than the loss avoided from pruning the truly bad accounts, the overall CLD strategy would be detrimental to the portfolio's profitability.

Thus, it is important to find a balance between loss mitigation and customer retention. This requires some analysis of the actual portfolio. Let's look at how the analysis is conducted in Example 9-1.

Example 9-1 Profitability of CLD by Loss Rate and Attrition Rate

A risk analyst was able to develop a strategy to identify 100 accounts with an annual # Loss Rate of 15%, i.e., 15 accounts out of the 100 are expected to become charge-offs after 12 months. The analyst now tries to estimate the impact by reducing the credit line of all 100 accounts.

Loss Savings

Historical data shows that, without CLD, the 15 bad ones from the 100 target accounts would have doubled their balance from an average of $3,000 to an average of $6,000. Thus, the loss savings from pruning bad accounts is 15 * ($6,000 – $3,000) = 15 * $3,000 = $45,000.

Lost Revenue

This would be the first time this lender introduces a CLD strategy, and thus there is no historical data to measure the attrition. An assumption of the balance attrition rate will be used.

If there is no balance attrition, the 85 good accounts will generate an annual revenue of 85 * $3,000 * 16% APR = $255,000 * 16% = $40,800.

Not having any balance attrition is probably an unrealistic expectation. The analyst then performed some examination to see what would happen if there were to be a 5% balance attrition from the good accounts.

With an assumed 5% attrition rate, the lost revenue from good accounts is 5% * Total Revenue $40,800 = $2,040.

The 5% attrition rate might be too optimistic. The analyst went ahead to list more scenarios where the attrition rate ranges from 10% to 50%, as shown in Exhibit 9-1.

Exhibit 9-1   CLD Profitability under Different Attrition Scenarios

$ Loss Savings from CLD	Revenue from Good Balance @ 16%	Attrition Rate of Good Balance	Lost Revenue due to Attrition	$ Loss Saving Net of $ Lost Revenue
$45,000	$40,800	5%	$2,040	$42,960
$45,000	$40,800	10%	$4,080	$40,920
$45,000	$40,800	20%	$8,160	$36,840
$45,000	$40,800	30%	$12,240	$32,760
$45,000	$40,800	40%	$16,320	$28,680
$45,000	$40,800	50%	$20,400	$24,600

Profitability

With the loss savings and lost revenue, the analyst calculated the profitability under each scenario in the last column of Exhibit 9-1.

The exhibit shows that the overall profitability gradually decreases with an increase in the attrition rate. However, even with a 50% balance attrition rate, the overall profitability still is $24,600. Based on this, the analyst was confident that the CLD strategy should be profitable for the portfolio.

After the strategy was presented and approved, the risk analyst implemented the CLD strategy on 20% of the portfolio. The plan was to test the assumption of attrition rate before rolling it out on a larger scale.

9.1.2   Decision Elements

The typical decision elements used in a CLD strategy include:

- ☑ Account Status Code
- ☑ VIP or Private Banking Indicator — typically used for the purpose of exclusion
- ☑ Time Since Last Credit Line Change — accounts with recent line change typically are excluded, such as:
  - ▸ CLI occurrence in the past 12 months
  - ▸ CLD occurrence in the past 6 months
- ☑ Delinquency Status
- ☑ Recent Payment Delinquency History
- ☑ Existing Credit Line
- ☑ Balance
- ☑ Open to Buy
- ☑ Months on Book
- ☑ Credit Bureau Score - the latest refreshed score
- ☑ Behavior Score
- ☑ Bankruptcy Score
- ☑ CLD Score
- ☑ Spend Level
- ☑ Banking Relationship — see Section 7.2.1 for details

CLD Score

In order to effectively identify the targets of the CLD, some lenders also resort to the development of a CLD score. A CLD score typically identifies accounts that are most likely become money losers in next 12-24 months and also have enough open-to-buy to reduce.

As a CLD score can combine many internal and external variables, its adoption will reduce the number of decision elements used in the credit strategy, thus saving the real estate of additional decision elements and simplifying the strategy structure.

9.1.3   CLD Actions

For identified high-risk accounts, the limit can be decreased all the way to the existing balance, with a room of about 2% of the balance to accommodate accrued interest and fees. Then, the amount is rounded up to the nearest $100 or $500.

If the assessed risk is high but not overly high, the CLD action could be a percentage of the existing credit line, such as a 50% limit reduction or a 30% limit reduction, still with balance plus a small amount of room as the floor.

Alternatively, the CLD action can be a fixed amount reduction, such as a $2,000 decrease or a $3,000 decrease, again with the balance plus a small amount of room as the floor.

Exhibit 9-2 shows the assignment of various CLD actions based on dollar loss rate.

Exhibit 9-2   Sample CLD Actions

$ Loss Rate	CLD Action
< 10.00%	No CLD
10.00% - 11.99%	30% Limit Decrease
12.00% - 14.99%	50% Limit Decrease
15.00+%	CLD to Balance

For accounts delinquent beyond 1 cycle, the authorization capability has typically been taken away. Thus the action of a CLD is not that urgent at these stages. The best time to exert a CLD is when the account is still current or in cycle 1, during which they are still able to transact.

Nevertheless, CLD actions do happen to accounts at a later stage of delinquency — more as a penalizing action instead of a preventative action.

9.1.4 Adverse Action Letter

Much like in origination, the regulation requires that a lender issue an adverse action letter to notify the customer of the CLD action, as well as the reasons for the action.

If a credit bureau score is used as part of the CLD decision, the score value, score reasons, credit bureau name, and credit bureau contact information all need to be included in the letter.

Similarly, if a behavior score is used as part of the decision, the score reasons need to be displayed as well.

Tip: for an internally developed CLD score that does not have score reasons, or when it takes too much effort to build CLD score reason codes into the letter system, you can place the credit bureau score and behavior score after the CLD score in the CLD strategy. This way, you can leverage their existing score reason codes, which are typically already built into the letter system.

9.1.5 Sample CLD Strategy

Exhibit 9-3 shows a simplified CLD strategy as an example.

The strategy starts with recent limit change activity — only accounts without a limit change in the last 6 months are considered as potential CLD targets. This condition avoids the situation that an account receives a CLD too frequently.

Then, accounts with a current delinquency cycle <= 1 will go down the branch on the left. If an account has a CLD score

< 500 and credit bureau score < 700, it will receive a 30% decrease to its existing credit line.

Exhibit 9-3 A Simple CLD Strategy

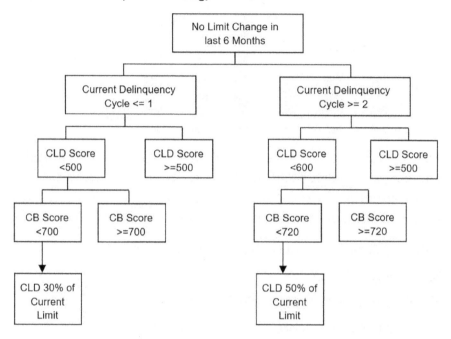

Accounts with a current delinquency cycle >= 2 will go down the branch on the right. If an account has a CLD Score < 600 and a credit bureau score < 720, it will receive a 50% decrease to its existing credit line.

Please note that as the delinquency grows, the risk score cut-offs are higher and the CLD action becomes more aggressive.

9.1.6 CLD Monitoring

Lenders typically closely track the # and $ of the limit reduction under the CLD strategy. Exhibit 9-4 shows such a sample graph.

Exhibit 9-4 # and % CLD Occurrence out of Total Accounts

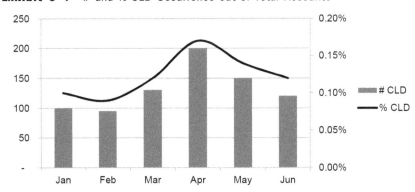

For a portfolio with large volume growth via acquisition campaign or portfolio acquisition, it would make sense to pay more attention to the percentage of CLD. The percentage can be calculated out of total open accounts or total active accounts.

Other typically used CLD tracking reports include:

☑ Average $ CLD

☑ Percentage of $ CLD / Credit Limit

☑ # CLD by Risk Score — See Exhibit 9-5

☑ # CLD by Delinquency Cycle

☑ # CLD by Months on Book

Exhibit 9-5 # and % CLD Occurrence out of Total Accounts

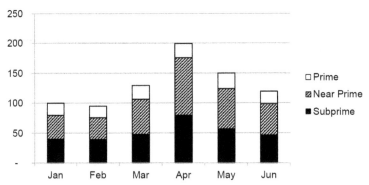

Prime: FICO 700+; Near Prime: FICO 620-699; Subprime: FICO<620

9.2 High-risk Inactive Closure

Many revolving accounts become inactive over time. Inactive means the account has no purchase, no balance, no interest, or fee charged for an extended period of time.

For these inactive accounts, it is a good practice to monitor their credit bureau scores on a regular basis and close down those with credit bureau scores drifting into a low range.

How does an inactive account pose a risk to the credit portfolio?

Even though your credit card or line of credit has not been used lately, a customer experiencing financial difficulty very likely will tap your credit line eventually. Once that happens, it is fairly hard to mitigate the risk since the balance often ramps up quickly.

Thus, the best time to act is as soon as you identify the customer's heightened risk based on the credit bureau data — take away the credit exposure while you can.

Inactivity

How inactive does an account need to become before the high-risk inactive closure strategy kicks in? There are several scenarios here.

Never Active

For accounts that were never activated and the risk level is high, you could close the account after it is open for over 12 months.

Inactive 12+ Months

For accounts that used to be active at one point of time and then become inactive 12 months or even longer, it is a pretty standard practice to close the account if the credit bureau score deteriorates.

Inactive 7-11 Months

It is relatively aggressive to take action on accounts that just become inactive for more than 6 months and less than 12 months.

However, if your risk analysis justifies the action and it is important for you to manage the portfolio risk down at the moment, there is nothing wrong in including this segment in your closure strategy.

For a full-service bank, you might want to spare the closure actions from those with a long-term banking relationship or those with a large amount of funds in their banking accounts. Some empirical analysis based on banking data should be able to tell you where to draw the line.

Score Cut-off

The particular credit bureau score cut-off for each inactive segment can be derived by conducting a risk analysis of your portfolio. Profitability is another key metric that should be incorporated into the strategy's design.

Consistency with Origination Strategy

Your high-risk closure strategy also needs to align with your origination strategy.

One question you want to ask is, "If the cardholder I close down today applies for a new credit card right away, would that application be approved?"

If the answer is "yes," then your closure strategy is probably too severe, or your origination strategy needs to be tightened up. A more coordinated analysis with your colleague who is responsible for the origination strategy might be needed.

If the answer is "no," then it is a confirmation that the account is out of your portfolio risk appetite from the front end, so it should be closed down.

9.3 Low-risk Inactive Closure

It's easy to understand why you would close high-risk inactive accounts, but why close low-risk inactive accounts?

This is because some lenders assign an overall exposure cap at the product level. An unused credit line is counted toward the total exposure cap and could thus stop the portfolio from growing before the exposure cap is lifted. Capital is also allocated for an undrawn credit line.

Thus, it is better to reallocate the unused exposure to brand new accounts or eligible existing accounts that are more likely to use it.

Once an account becomes inactive for two years or more, the likelihood that it will become active again is very small. For those that do reactivate, the issuer needs to be aware of the "adverse selection" effect — it is usually the high-risk account holders who will reactivate the cards as they possibly exhaust other financing options.

Inactivity

As some customers tend to use selected credit cards only during the holiday season each year, retail card issuers would typically wait to see at least 18 months of inactivity before closing down the low-risk accounts.

Bankcards typically wait to see at least 24 months of inactivity before closing down low-risk accounts. This includes "never active" accounts.

Communication

In order to remind customers to use their credit accounts, it is a good practice to send out a reminder via letter or email. This reminder could be sent 3 months before the intended closure date, so customers have enough time to receive the communication and respond.

The message on the communication could be a simple "use it or lose it" text. If a customer still does not respond by using the account, you can safely assume that the customer has no interest in using this account anymore and close it down on schedule.

Remember to check with your regional regulations, as such a notification before a long-term inactive closure might be mandatory or optional. In the case of optional pre-closure communication, another factor to consider is whether the budget for the notification can be better used elsewhere, especially for mail notifications.

9.4 Exposure Reduction Report

With multiple limit reduction strategies in place, it is a good practice for lenders to track the total exposure reduction on a monthly basis.

In Exhibit 9-6, a lender breaks down the monthly total dollar credit limit reduction into 5 main categories.

☑ CLD

☑ Low-Risk Inactive Closure

☑ High-Risk Inactive Closure

☑ Current Revoke — current accounts that are closed by the lender

☑ Delinquent Revoke — delinquent accounts that are closed by the lender

Exhibit 9-6 Monthly $ Exposure Reduction by Strategy ($ Million)

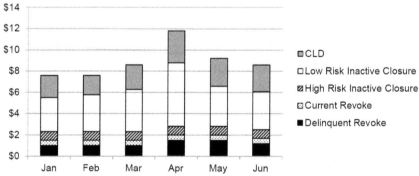

Having such a report helps show the overall impact from various limit reduction strategies. It also helps to project the monthly volume going forward.

Because a small percentage of customers will call in to complain about the limit reduction or account closure, the volume forecast can help customer service and underwriting teams plan resources accordingly. Any major change in related strategies should be communicated to these stakeholders as well.

Other exposure reduction reports include:

- ☑ % of Total $ Exposure Reduction / Total Portfolio Exposure
- ☑ $ Exposure Reduction by Risk Score
- ☑ $ Exposure Reduction by Delinquency Cycle
- ☑ $ Exposure Reduction by Month-on-Book

9.5 Reinstatement

After accounts are subject to CLD or account closure, some customers might call or write to request that the limit be reinstated and their account be reopened.

At this time, the underwriting team or the risk team should perform another quick risk assessment of the account, taking any new information into consideration, such as a payment behavior after the CLD or account closure, the overall banking relationship, and a customer's special circumstance.

If, upon assessment, the risk is deemed low enough, the account can have its limit reinstated or be reopened.

Log and Review Reinstatement Requests

It is a good practice to always log the customers' complaints and reinstatement requests in response to various types of exposure reduction actions.

By reviewing the log after you accumulate a few months' data, you might be able to find some opportunities to fine-tune the strategies to make them more precise. Example 9.2 illustrates the value of such a review.

Example 9.2 Review of Reinstatement Requests Enhanced Strategy

A full service bank recently implemented a CLD strategy for its credit card portfolio. By reviewing the customers' reinstatement requests over the previous 3 months, the risk team found that 50% of the requests were from bank customers who have a long-term deposit account relationship.

Further analysis revealed that the tenure and balance of deposit accounts can further segment out a portion of previous CLD targets that have low-risk performance. By incorporating the latest finding in a modified CLD strategy, the lender was able to effectively reduce the number of customer complaints and avoid alienating valuable bank customers.

Performance of Reinstated Accounts

Another good exercise is to review the performance of accounts that have been reinstated — after 12 months, for example. This should help validate the assumptions adopted at the time of reinstatement and detect potential bias.

What is learned from the performance review can be used to develop more detailed guidelines regarding which customers are qualified for reinstatement and in which scenarios. The learnings can also enhance the original limit reduction strategies so that complaints and reinstatement requests can be minimized in the first place.

Chapter 10
Collections

Whether for a revolving credit product such as credit card or for an installment loan, the accountholder is typically required to make a payment each month.

If a customer fails to make the payment required by the specified payment due date, the account becomes delinquent or past due. This is where collection comes in.

Lenders use different channels such as phone calls or letters to reach out to delinquent customers and collect required payments — this process is called collection.

In Section 10.1, we will focus on the collection strategy for delinquent accounts. Delinquency collection is the scenario in which the vast majority of collection activities take place.

Besides collections being enacted due to delinquency, they can also be performed on non-delinquent accounts. Section 10.2 covers overlimit collections and Section 10.3 introduces pre-delinquency collections.

10.1 Delinquency Collections

Delinquency can happen for a number of reasons. Not every delinquent account needs a lender's collection activity right away, as some accounts catch up on payments on their own.

For example, Joe went on an extended vacation and missed paying that month's credit card bill. Joe's credit card company noticed that he had paid his bills in a timely manner over the previous two years, and therefore did not initiate any collection activity immediately. They planned to call Joe only if no payment had arrived during the ensuing 15 days. When Joe returned from vacation 5 days later, he saw the bill and made a payment at once.

A lot of collection activities are carried out by collectors. As the resources of collectors are always finite, the decisions in collections essentially are **who to contact** and **which contact method to use**. Next, let's look at how these decisions are made.

10.1.1 Collection Strategy

The rules that determine which delinquent accounts will receive which collection treatment and which contact method will be used are called a collection strategy. A collection strategy is usually owned by the credit risk team, while the actual collection activities are carried out by the collections operations team.

A list of delinquent accounts is downloaded daily, as determined by the collection strategy. This list is available for collections operations to work on. A collections operations department consists of a team of collectors who specialize in different collection tactics. A collection operations team typically operates out of a call center environment, as the phone is still the primary contact method for collections.

However, in the case of phone collections, not every account on the list will necessarily get worked on during that day. This is because the list is sometimes too long for collectors to work through in one day. In this case, the collection operations team will decide which accounts get worked on first and when.

Please note that even though the credit risk team might have recommendations in terms of which accounts should be called and how frequently, the actual outbound calls are within the control of the collection operations team.

Thus, collections are a very dynamic process with the final actions driven by both collection strategy and collection operations. This chapter will just focus on the collection strategy, since this is the typical decision area of a credit risk team.

Collection strategies are quite different at each stage of delinquency. Next, let's look at each main delinquency stage.

10.1.2 Delinquency Stages

Early Stage Collections

Early stage collections usually refer to collections on accounts delinquent within the first 90 days. In delinquency, every 30 day period is counted as one cycle or one bucket. Accounts delinquent 1–29 days are called cycle 1 or bucket 1 accounts, accounts delinquent 30–59 days are called cycle 2 or bucket 2 accounts, and so on.

At the early stage, it is important to distinguish accounts that are likely to catch up with payments on their own (also known as "self-cure") or just with a quick reminder, from those that are very likely to roll forward to late stage delinquency.

As the vast majority of early stage accounts are delinquent within the first 60 days, and most of them will be able to catch up with payments, the precious collections resources should be allocated to those with a high likelihood of rolling forward into late stage delinquency.

Late Stage Collections

Once accounts become 90+ days delinquent, which means they are in Cycle 4+, there is a high probability that these accounts will eventually become credit losses. Credit losses, also called charge-offs, are usually defined as accounts reaching 180+ days delinquent, which means the accounts have missed six monthly payments, and are thus classified as bad debt.

At the late stage, the main objective of collections is to collect payment from the seriously delinquent accounts in order to stop them from continuing to roll forward into charge-offs.

Late stage accounts need to be segmented by the payments potentially being able to be collected, so the collection team can focus on those accounts that can make the most payments.

In the case of a small credit portfolio, there might not be enough late stage delinquent accounts to have a meaningful segmentation. Sometimes a single collector is able to work through all the late stage accounts within a single day. Nevertheless, it is still important to know which accounts have a better chance of making payments so they can be prioritized.

Recovery

Once an account becomes a charge-off, the loss is recognized in the accounting books. However, collection efforts on these accounts do not stop there.

A lender can continue to collect the bad debt by itself. This process is called "recovery." The cumulative recovery rate (total payments collected divided by the charge-off balance) could reach a range of 10% to 15%, which is a sizable stream of cash inflow that helps reduce the gross loss amount.

Instead of collecting the charge-off debt by itself, a lender could also choose to outsource the recovery activity or sell the bad debt to a company that specializes in recovery operations.

These recovery companies specialize in collecting on charge-off debt. They purchase the bad debts from different lenders with a heavily discounted price such as a few cents on the dollar.

For example, if the bad debt is sold to the recovery companies at 3% of the book value, that could still leave a revenue opportunity of 7%–12% (as a percentage of the initial bad debt) for the recovery company. All payments collected from the recovery process, minus the operational cost, become the profit earned by these recovery companies.

10.1.3 Decision Elements

Typical decision elements used in a collection strategy include:

- ☑ Days Delinquent or Cycle Delinquent
- ☑ Account Status Code
- ☑ Months on Book
- ☑ Recency of Payment — how many days since the last payment was made
- ☑ Credit Limit
- ☑ Current Balance
- ☑ Utilization
- ☑ Collections Score
- ☑ Credit Bureau Score - the latest refreshed score
- ☑ Behavior Score
- ☑ Balance at Risk — balance expected to become bad per risk score
- ☑ Delinquency History — for example:
  - ▸ Number of Times 1, 2, or 3+ cycles delinquent in last 12 months
  - ▸ Maximum Delinquency in the last 12 months
- ☑ Phone Indicator — good phone vs. bad phone
- ☑ Mail Indicator — good mailing address vs. bad mailing address
- ☑ Promise-to-Pay Indicator
- ☑ Special Payment Plan Indicator
- ☑ Banking Relationship — see Section 7.2.1 for details

10.1.4 Collection Actions

There are multiple actions available in collections. Depending on a particular account's risk level and delinquency stage, one or more collection actions could be deployed.

Statement Message

On a monthly statement, a message can be printed to remind the customer to pay the minimum payment due.

Since this message piggybacks on the existing statement, there is no increased cost for the lender. However, the problem is that many accountholders do not pay any attention to messages within a statement.

Some lenders use bold or red type in order to draw the customer's attention to these messages. This tactic is better than using the regular black text.

Phone Call

The most commonly used collection action is a phone call. All accounts eligible for a collection call, as determined by the collection strategy, are loaded into a collection dialer. The dialer is a powerful tool for dialing the list automatically. If the phone at the customer's end is picked up, it is connected with a live collector right away. The collector can have a conversation with the customer, understanding their financial situation, and get a promise to pay or work out a payment plan.

It is worth noting that the U.S. restricts the use of automatic dialers on cellular phone numbers[1]. Lenders typically purchase services from third parties to distinguish landline vs. cellular phone numbers and deploy different dialing strategies.

Letter

A letter is another commonly used contact method for collections. Depending on the stage and risk level of the delinquency, there could be as many as 10–20 collection letters in use with different verbiages.

The tone of a letter used for early stage delinquent accounts is usually fairly soft, as it is just meant as a reminder.

The tone of letters gradually becomes harsher as the number of days of delinquency increases. To motivate a customer to pay, the letter often cites the negative consequences of missing payments, such as damage to the consumer's credit report or losing access to revolving credit.

Text Message and Email

With increasing digitalization, text messages and emails are gaining popularity as additional communication channels with consumers. With the new debt collections rules passed by the CFPB in October 2020[2], these two channels are expected to get used more for colections as well.

Skip Tracing

Sometimes a customer has changed his or her phone number without notifying the lender, so there is no valid phone number that can be used to reach the customer.

Such accounts can be handed over to a specialized skip tracing team that uses specialized skip tracing tools from vendors to locate and contact these customers.

Settlement

Sometime a customer is too financially stretched to make a payment, and a charge-off will most likely happen. In this case, it is in the lender's interest to make a settlement offer to the consumer to request only a portion of the total debt to be paid.

For example, a lender sends out the following settlement offer to selected late stage delinquent customers: if the customer can make a payment of 60% of the total outstanding debt, the lender will forgo the other 40%.

This will provide the consumer with an incentive to come up with the payment in order to receive the relief of a good portion of the debt. For the lender, it is better to receive some payment than nothing.

Pre-Legal Collections and Legal Collections

For accounts with large outstanding balances, the lender could engage a law firm to take legal action against the cardholders.

Before getting to that stage, the lender usually sends a pre-legal collection letter 10–50 days before the expected charge-off date. The idea is to remind delinquent customers to treat the outstanding debt with high priority and have them call back to arrange the payment or work out a payment plan.

After an account becomes a charge-off, the legal action needs to follow through. A list of charge-off accounts will be sent to the law firm that has been contracted to start the legal collection process.

In Practice: Combined Actions

In a collection strategy, each individual node of the decision tree is usually assigned with a set of collection actions. Each action is connected to a particular timing within the current delinquency cycle.

Next, let's look at two examples — one in early stage delinquency and the other in late stage.

Example 10-1 Early Stage Collection Actions

> For an early stage delinquent account in Cycle 1 (1–29 days delinquent), Exhibit 10-1 shows the collection actions assigned as the following:
>
> ▸ On account cycle day, when the statement is generated, print statement message 101.
>
> ▸ If no payment is received by day 10 (10 days later), the collection letter 105 will be sent.

▸ If still no payment is received by day 20, the account will be put into the calling queue 03 so collectors will call this account. The priority assigned to this calling queue is "medium."

Exhibit 10-1 Collections Actions Assigned to Early Stage Delinquent Accounts

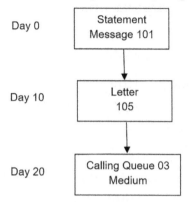

Example 10-2 Late Stage Collection Actions

For a late stage delinquent account entering cycle 5 (120 days delinquent), Exhibit 10-2 shows the collection actions assigned as the following:

▸ On account cycle day when the statement is generated, print statement message 501.

▸ On the same day, send out the collection letter 510.

▸ On the same day, the account is put in calling queue 50, which is high priority.

Exhibit 10-2 Collections Actions Assigned to a Late Stage Delinquent Account

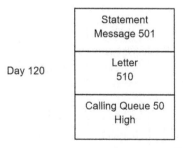

Because a cycle 5 account is very likely to become a charge-off, the letter and collection call actions are not held back.

10.1.5 Sample Collection Strategy

Exhibit 10-3 shows a sample early stage collection strategy for cycle 1 accounts.

If there is no payment ever on the account, it means that the account fails the very first payment due. This is a high risk flag, so such accounts are separated out as first payment default.

For accounts that have a history of payment and the outstanding balance is less than $100, the delinquency is most likely due to oversight on the part of the customer. Such accounts are segmented into a small balance collections queue.

Delinquent accounts with a balance >= $100 are further segmented into high/medium/low risk segments, based on the balance and collection score.

Exhibit 10-3 A Sample Collection Strategy

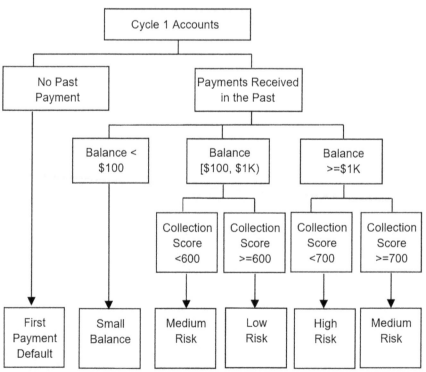

Based on assessed risk levels, different collection actions are assigned to each segment, as listed in Exhibit 10-4.

Exhibit 10-4 Sample Collection Actions

Segment	Collection Actions
First Payment Default	Satement message. Day 1 dialer queue with high call intensity. Day 5 collection letter 100.
Small Balance	Statement message.
Low Risk	Satement message. Day 15 collection letter 101. Day 20 dialer queue with low call intensity.
Medium Risk	Satement message. Day 10 collection letter 102. Day 15 dialer queue with medium call intensity.
High Risk	Satement message. Day 5 letter 103. Day 5 dialer queue with high call intensity.

10.1.6 Performance Measurement

Measurement of Delinquency Collection Strategy

For pre charge-off collections, there might be a specific objective for each delinquent bucket, such as an increased cure rate or a reduced bad rate down the road. However, a holistic approach should be taken to measure a collections strategy by tracking the balance flow from cycle 1 all the way to charge-off six months later.

Please note that the measurement does not start with current accounts, as the delinquency entry rate (roll rate from current accounts to cycle 1 accounts) is outside the control of collections. Only when an account becomes delinquent in cycle 1, does it enter the arena of collection strategy.

Next, let's look at an example in which 2 collection strategies are compared.

Example 10-1 Aggressive Collection Strategy Did Not Pay Off

With the objective of tackling rising delinquency and loss, a lender introduced a new challenger collection strategy to 40% of the portfolio six months ago.

The challenger strategy puts cycle 1 accounts into dialer queues 10 days earlier on average, as compared with the champion. In addition, letters with more demanding tones are deployed under the challenger; they are sent out 8 days earlier than the champion, on average.

To evaluate the effectiveness of the challenger strategy, the risk team calculated the roll rates through different delinquency buckets all the way to charge-off for both strategies, as Exhibit 10-5 shows.

The tracking shows that the more aggressive actions in the early stage did lower the dollar roll rate from cycle 1 to 2 under the challenger strategy, which is 28.1% vs. 30.0% under the champion. Similarly, for the dollar roll rate from cycle 2 to cycle 3, the challenger has 71.5% vs. champion's 72.0%.

However, the subsequent roll rates during mid and late stages all deteriorated under the challenger. At the end of a 6-month performance period, the multiplication of all the continuous roll rates shows that the challenger had 15.3% of cycle 1 balance ending up as loss, which actually is about 20 bps more than the 15.1% under the champion. The challenger was not as effective as the champion.

Exhibit 10-5 Performance Comparison between Two Strategies

$ Roll Rates Under the Champion Strategy

Last Month	Current Month 1	2	3	4	5	6	C/O	
1		30.0%						
2			72.0%					
3				86.5%				
4					88.0%			
5						94.0%		
6							98.0%	15.1%
C/O								

$ Roll Rates Under the Challenger Strategy

Last Month	Current Month 1	2	3	4	5	6	C/O	
1		28.1%						
2			71.5%					
3				89.0%				
4					90.5%			
5						96.5%		
6							98.0%	15.3%
C/O								

This example illustrates that it is important to have a holistic review of a collection strategy. By only looking at the roll rates of early stage delinquency, the challenger strategy is seen to be working great.

However, the early success of the challenger was most likely based on assigning many collection resources to those low risk accounts, which are likely to self-cure or cure with just a gentle reminder. At the same time, the high risk accounts probably did not receive the collections efforts that they warranted.

Thus, a collections strategy needs to optimize the collections efforts based on an individual customer's risk profile. Aggressive collections do not always pay off.

Measurement of Recovery

For post-charge-off collections or recoveries, the cumulative recovery (payment) rate against the original charge-off amount is often used to evaluate the effectiveness of the recovery efforts.

Exhibit 10-6 shows the 24-month performance of three quarterly charge-off vintages. The cumulative dollar recovery rates at the end of 24 months are very close. However, the rate has deteriorated slightly from the Q1 vintage to the Q3 vintage. Further analysis is recommended to understand what has caused the slide in recovery performance.

Exhibit 10-6 $ Recovery Rate Curves by Charge-off Vintage

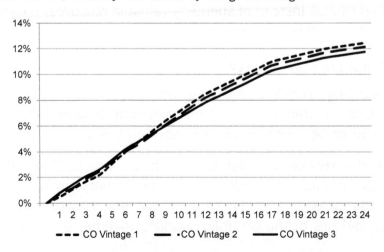

10.1.6 Outsourcing and Portfolio Sales

Outsourcing

Any of the collection operations mentioned earlier can be outsourced to a third party who specializes in collections call center operations, skip tracing, recovery collections, legal collection, etc.

In the case of outsourcing, the performance still needs to be closely monitored by the lender, which is the owner of the credit portfolio. Frequent communication between the lender and the outsourcing operator is necessary in order to address any issue observed in the dynamic collection environment.

Portfolio Sales

Instead of outsourcing or collecting past due amounts by itself, a lender can also sell part of the delinquent portfolio before or after charge-off.

Usually, the portfolio being sold is the one that is most difficult to collect, such as a skip tracing portfolio before the charge-off, late stage accounts with a low probability of receiving payments, or the charge-offs.

Depending on the lender's objective and its own strengths, it sometimes makes sense to sell the challenging portfolio and free up capital, instead of spending valuable resources collecting on its own without achieving the desired results.

Outsourcing or Sales?

Outsourcing requires an onboarding process. With more emphasis on third-party risk management, it does take some effort to bring a new service provider on board.

Once the service provider is brought on board, there is still a need for a lender to actively manage the outsourcing activity, such as helping the service provider get familiar with the characteristics of the portfolio, working together to design and monitor the operations, creating incentives for the operating staff, and regularly reviewing key metrics.

If the performance of the outsourced portfolio is unsatisfactory, a lender can choose to change the service provider or bring the portfolio back in-house.

The potential risk is that it usually takes a while to find out that the service provider's performance is subpar compared to the original expectation. If that happens, there are definitely lost opportunities and unfavorable economics for the portfolio owner.

Compared with outsourcing, portfolio sales is relatively simpler. The proceeds from sales bring in revenue immediately, instead of waiting for the funds collected in the coming months and years.

However, there is still a reputational risk for the lender who originated the loan. In the consumers' eyes, the debt is always associated with the lender, even though the ownership changes hands behind the scenes. Thus, lenders really need to be careful when choosing the buyer of bad debts and ensure that the collection practice regulations are all fully complied with.

10.2 Overlimit Collections

If an account is overlimit and delinquent, it falls into the scope of delinquent collections. In case an account is just overlimit but still current, special collection can still be conducted.

Allowing an account to go overlimit is meant to provide convenience to customers at the time of purchase. However, the expectation from the lender is that the cardholder should bring the balance down to within the limit by the end of the current billing cycle (when the next statement is generated).

If the account remains overlimit at the time of billing and is not delinquent, the lender can assign a special collections team to such an account to perform overlimit collection.

The fact that an account remains in overlimit status and is not able to bring the balance down is a risk signal. Therefore, it is good risk practice to have a strategy and process in place to work on these overlimit accounts.

The main targets of overlimit collection are the high risk ones. Such accounts usually carry a large overlimit amount, have a low behavior score and/or low credit bureau score.

Similar to delinquent collections, actions implemented with overlimit collection include:

☑ Statement message

☑ Letter

☑ Collection phone call

For overlimit collections, the call script is different from those used in delinquency collections. It is usually used just to ask the cardholder to bring the balance down to within the existing credit limit.

10.3 Pre-delinquency Collections

The delinquency status starts on the cycle date. In practice, the payment due date on the statement is usually a few days before the next cycle date. Thus, an account that fails to make the minimum required payment by the payment due date is not officially delinquent yet, as there is the possibility that the payment arrives before the next cycle date.

However, the fact that the minimum required payment is missed by the payment due date is a clear signal that the account is more likely to become delinquent a few days later.

Thus, a more proactive collection tactic is to collect on some of these accounts that miss the payment by the payment due date, before they officially become delinquent on the impending cycle date.

Maybe such an account has been late with payments lately, or recently became late on external loans. There is a lot of internal and external information that a lender can search through and predict which accounts are most likely to become delinquent.

Once the potentially delinquent accounts are identified, a soft collection call can be initiated — to remind the customer of a payment being due now and the potential consequences of late payments.

For some customers who always have trouble making timely payments, it is also an opportunity to help the customer set up an automatic payment plan.

Prior to Payment Due Date

With the advancement of technology, lenders can initiate contact even days before the payment due date, via an email or a text message. Both communication methods are low cost and are perceived as less invasive by customers.

Regardless of the timing and contact methods, all of these serve the purpose of mitigating potential delinquency before it becomes realized.

Chapter 11
Reissue

11.1 Overview

Online Reissue vs. Batch Reissue

Sometimes, credit card customers' physical cards (also called "plastics") become lost or get stolen. In this case, they just need to call their card issuer to get new plastics sent to them. The process of issuing a new plastic to the cardholder under this scenario is called online reissue, as the reissue decision is made in real-time when the customer speaks with the customer service representative.

Besides online reissue under the lost/stolen scenario, every credit card is expected to go through a regular reissue process toward the end of the expiration date of the plastic card. You can find the last effective month and year embossed or printed on the physical card with a format of MM/YY. A credit card is valid until the very last day of the month of expiration.

Because there are often many cards expiring on the same day, this regular reissue process is also referred to as a batch reissue. This is a unique decision process that pertains to credit cards and some of the VISA/MasterCard branded debit cards (which can be used as credit cards online).

As most new plastics are reissued via batch reissue, this chapter provides more details on this process and the related strategy.

11.2 Batch Reissue

Under batch reissue, there are essentially two decisions for the card issuer to make for each expiring account. The first is **whether to reissue a new plastic or not**. The second is **how long the validity period of the new plastic will be**. Next, we will look at how these two decisions are made, individually.

Reissue Decision

Near the expiration date, the card issuer will have access to a lot of information on a particular account, such as internal behavior history and external credit bureau information.

With all the information available, the card issuer can make a fair assessment of the risk associated with the account. If it is deemed too risky and unprofitable for the lender, it makes business sense for the lender to let the relationship end naturally on the impending expiration date and no new plastic will be issued.

A non-issuance example would be an account cycle 2+ delinquent, i.e., at least two payments behind at time of expiration.

The accounts that will not be reissued a new plastic only represent a small percentage of the total expiring accounts. Especially if robust CLD and account closure strategies had been steadily running for a while, most high risk accounts would have already been identified and dealt with.

Reissue Period Decision

For the vast majority of accounts that would receive the new plastics, the card issuer has a chance to decide how long the new reissue period will be, i.e., what the new expiration date on the new plastic will be.

The length of the reissue period should be determined by the risk level of the account. Exhibit 11-1 shows such an example.

For low risk accounts that have an expected annual dollar loss rate <= 2.00%, the card issuer can go ahead to issue a 48-month plastic. If a 24-month plastic is issued instead, these accounts would most likely be reissued a new plastic two years later, anyway.

By issuing a 48-month plastic instead of two 24-month plastics successively, the issuer saves the reissue cost of one card, which includes the cost of plastics, chip, envelope, and postage. This cost could add up quickly, especially for a large card portfolio, which could have millions of accounts.

Exhibit 11-1 Sample Reissue Periods by Risk Level

Annualized $ Loss Rate	Reissue Period
<= 2.00%	48 Months
2.01% - 4.00%	36 Months
4.01% - 8.00%	24 Months
8.01% - 10.00%	18 Months
10.01% - 14.00%	12 Months
14.01+%	No Reissue

For medium risk accounts with an expected annual dollar loss rate of from 4.01% to 8.00%, their risk and profitability merit issuing new plastics and the relationships should be continued. However, there is a larger chance that things could 'go south' for a cardholder's financial capability in a period of four years. Thus, it is in the best interest of the issuer to issue a shorter period, such as 2 years. Then the issuer can evaluate again at the end of year 2 whether the relationship should continue.

For risk between medium and low levels (annual dollar loss rate 2.01%–4.00%), the reissue period can be set as 36 months. For risk higher than medium but not as bad as non-reissuance accounts, the reissue period could be set as 18 months (annual dollar loss rate 4.01%–8.00%) and 12 months (annual dollar loss rate 10.01%–14.00%).

In summary, the reissue periods should be reversely correlated to the account's risk level. The lower the risk, the longer the reissue period; the higher the risk, the lower the reissue period.

11.3 Decision Elements

Typical decision elements used in a reissue strategy include:

- ☑ Days Delinquent or Cycles Delinquent
- ☑ Delinquency History in the Last 12 or 24 months
- ☑ Credit Bureau Score — the latest refreshed score
- ☑ Behavior Score
- ☑ Current Balance
- ☑ Utilization
- ☑ Month on Book
- ☑ Special Payment Plan Indicator
- ☑ Banking Relationship — see Section 7.2.1 for details

11.4 Monitoring Reports

Reissue Volume by Calendar Month

For operational purposes, it is always good to have the monthly reissue volume (the number of accounts and plastics expiring in a month) in the next 12 months available at hand. This will be used to plan how many new plastics should be ordered.

Customer service could also get a sense of inbound calls related to the inquiry of new plastics and call activation.

For a card portfolio that just booked a large volume of new accounts via a one-time acquisition campaign, there will be a spike in reissue volume a few years down the road, which is illustrated by the Scenario 1 curve in Exhibit 11-2.

Over time, as a portfolio becomes more seasoned, the monthly volume usually becomes smoother, which is easier to manage from an operational perspective. This would be the Scenario 2 curve in the same exhibit.

Exhibit 11-2 Illustrative Monthly Reissue Volumes

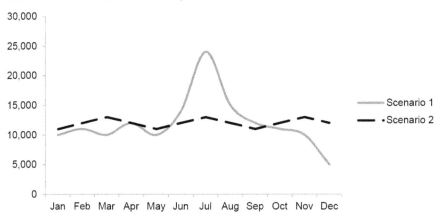

Reissue Volume by Period

It is also good to monitor the monthly reissue volume by the new reissue period, as shown in Exhibit 11-3. Under normal conditions, the distribution of various reissue periods should be fairly stable.

If, in a given month, the volume of one particular segment — say, reissues for 24-month periods — becomes too high, you probably want to check if there is any unintended strategy change or some other difference in reasoning.

Exhibit 11-3 Monthly Reissue Volume by Reissue Period

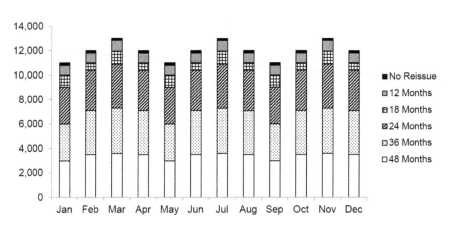

Average Risk Score by Reissue Period

For reissued accounts, the risk team usually tracks the quality of credit decisions by the average risk score associated with each reissue period, in order to make sure the scores rank order across different reissue periods and are stable over time.

Exhibit 11-4 shows the average credit bureau score of accounts reissued with different periods in each month. Overall, the average score lines are fairly stable. If there is any sudden spike or dip, further investigation can be conducted.

Exhibit 11-4 Average Credit Bureau Score by Reissue Period

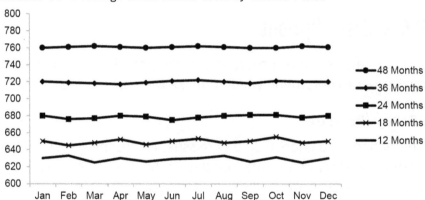

A similar graph can be plotted based on a behavior score.

Non-Reissuance Accounts

Non-reissuance accounts are typically monitored by the risk team as well. Exhibit 11-5 shows the distribution of non-reissued accounts by credit bureau score in each month.

The exhibit helps confirm that most non-reissuance accounts fall into near prime and subprime segments. Also, the percentage of non-reissuance is relatively stable from month to month.

Exhibit 11-5 Percentage of Non-Reissue by Credit Bureau Score

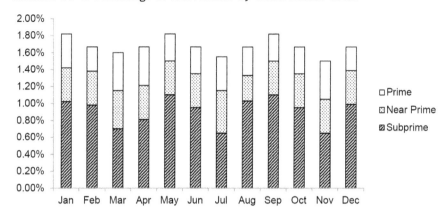

11.5 Reissue Options

A credit card issuance processor usually provides options to the card issuer to determine when to make the final reissue decision.

30-Day Reissue

One option is to choose 30-day reissue, i.e., running the reissue strategy 30 days before the last day of the month of expiration. If the expiration date is 05/21, or May 2021, the last day of the expiration month is May 31, 2021. Then, the reissue strategy will run one month prior, on April 30th, 2021.

The 30-day reissue will ensure that the decision is based on the information available as close as possible to the final expiration date. However, it does take time for the plastics vendor to prepare the plastics and mailers, so some accountholders might not be able to get the new plastic until during the last week of the reissue month, or in May 2021, in the example above.

If there is any delay during the mailing process, the cardholder will not have the new plastic in hand by the time the existing card expires, which could be quite an inconvenience — especially if the card is the primary payment tool for the customer. Also, it is inevitable that some customers will call into the call center to inquire about new cards, which would definitely drive up the inbound call volume.

60-Day Reissue

Another option is to choose 60-days reissue, i.e., running the reissue strategy 60 days before the last day of the month of expiration. In the same example above, if the expiration date is the last day of the expiration month, May 31, 2021, the reissue strategy will run on March 31, 2021, which is exactly two months prior to the expiration date.

If an account is qualified, the plastic will be sent out between 60 and 30 days prior to the last day of the month of expiration. This would allow enough time for the new plastic to travel and provide the cardholder the peace of mind of knowing that the issuer has not forgotten about them. The inbound call inquiries of new plastics would also be reduced.

For accounts that fail 60 days prior to the expiration date, they can usually get reevaluated 30 days prior to the expiration date. This provides an opportunity to reinstate some accounts. If the credit situation improves, the accounts can still be reissued with new plastics.

The converse is also possible, i.e., an account is qualified at 60 days prior, but the score drifts downward and it is no longer qualified 30 days prior to expiration. To address this risk, it is recommended that the lender set up the 60 days prior strategy a bit tighter — for example, the minimum credit bureau score might be 20 points higher. This essentially leaves the decision of accounts on the margin to the last possible date, which is 30 days prior.

Rank by Risk Score

The credit card issuance processor also provides options for the issuer to decide which accounts to mail the new plastics to first.

It is recommended that high credit score accounts are reissued first, so your credit exposure is associated with low risk accounts only. Alternatively, a lender can choose to send out plastics randomly in several batches.

You can work with your credit card processor to see exactly which options are available and how to set them up to meet your needs.

11.6 Authorization for new plastics

Although this topic is related to authorization, it is also closely related to newly reissued plastics. Thus, it is placed at the end of this chapter.

Traditionally reissued plastics would require cardholders to activate their cards, just as they receive their very first plastics when the account is opened. This is to make sure that the plastics have not fallen into the wrong hands.

In addition, if a customer calls in to activate the plastics, it presents the card issuer with an opportunity to cross-sell other products and services by connecting the cardholder with a live agent.

However, there are some lenders who choose to approve some authorizations associated with reissued plastics without activation.

Why is that?

This is because there are always some consumers who forget to activate the new plastics before using them. It is very possible that the old plastics have already expired, so this could be the only card that the customer has to make purchases with.

In order to provide a good customer experience, a lender can choose to approve some low-risk authorizations from the unactivated cards. A low risk example would be a two-dollar transaction at a coffee shop from a good credit customer.

When the transaction amount is large or from high risk merchants, the lender can always decline such authorizations and then effectively force the customer to activate the card.

The extent to which a lender should approve authorizations from unactivated reissue plastics depends on the issuer's overall risk appetite and business objective around the authorization approval rate, which is a big part of the customer experience.

To help make that decision, a card issuer should monitor how many declines are from non-activated reissue plastics, what the authorization amount distribution is, and typically from which merchants.

It is worth mentioning that some issuers have recently even forgone card activation altogether. To do so, they have robust fraud strategies in place that can effectively identify and decline high-risk authorizations associated with non-receipt fraud.

Chapter 12
Portfolio Stimulation Campaigns

Chapters 4–11 covered the main credit risk decision areas for a credit portfolio. Besides those, there are a few other tactics that are often deployed to stimulate the growth of the portfolio balance.

These tactics are used to different degrees at different financial institutions. They are often implemented as campaigns, instead of being constantly run on credit decision engines like the core credit risk strategies.

In this chapter, we will introduce a few common portfolio stimulation campaigns in the following sections.

☑ Section 12.1: Balance Transfer

☑ Section 12.2: Skip a Payment

☑ Section 12.3: Interest Only

12.1 Balance Transfer

Balance Transfer is a campaign in which a card issuer offers a special low interest rate to entice its existing cardholders to transfer their external balance to their accounts with the card issuer.

With the lower rate, balance transfer helps customers reduce their financial burden. For the card issuer, balance transfer is a great way to bring the customer's external balance in-house and grow its market share of total balance.

Balance transfer is a good example of a portfolio management tactic that is usually led by the business team and is not considered the core function of the risk management team. However, the risk team still needs to be closely involved in order for the lender to target the customers with appropriate risk levels and help the initiative achieve the intended business goals.

For a risk professional involved in a balance transfer campaign, it is important to understand the particular objectives of a given campaign. Sometimes the objectives might not be fully articulated by the business team, so you can help ensure that the campaign will be a success by asking some questions for the sake of clarification.

12.1.1 Balance Transfer Offer and Risk Appetite

The business team tends to test different APRs and balance transfer fees to see which offers are most attractive to customers. However, a 0% APR for 18 months with a 3% fee does not leave a lot of room for credit loss.

The very first question you want to ask is, "What is the profitability target the business team has in mind for this campaign?"

The implicit assumption is that a balance transfer campaign should make some kind of profit. After all, the credit business is for-profit and nobody wants to lose money.

Just understanding the ballpark number of expected profit will help you design the risk targeting criteria better.

In the meantime, please also be prepared to hear responses like "as much as possible." This does not provide the specific answer you were hoping for, but at least it confirms the objective — to maximize the profit from the campaign.

In either case, you would need to construct the risk criteria based on the overall portfolio risk appetite. The other key inputs include the expected response rate and average dollar balance transferred for each risk band.

If there are historical campaigns run on the portfolio already, you can analyze the most recent ones to obtain the empirical numbers to use. Otherwise, just input some assumptions and be ready to adjust, based on further conversation with the project team.

Let's look at Example 12.1 and see how the risk criteria are derived, based on risk appetite and the campaign's objectives.

Example 12.1 The Risk Criteria Design for a Balance Transfer Campaign

A card issuer plans to roll out another balance transfer campaign and the risk team has been engaged to provide the risk selection criteria.

The offer for the balance transfer campaign is a 3% balance transfer fee with a 3% APR for 12 months. This is the same offer used in a previous balance transfer campaign that was launched 12 months ago. Thus, the historical number of response rate and the average dollar balance transfer per responder can be used for analysis of the current campaign.

The card issuer has a risk appetite of 5% annual dollar loss rate. That means accounts with a credit bureau score of 660 and above are all safe to target. That was the risk criteria used in last year's campaign, as one of the objectives was to test the performance of different bands of risk.

The business team told the risk team that the objective of this campaign is to maximize profitability. With that in mind, the risk analyst who was assigned to this project began to construct an analysis by credit bureau score band.

First, the analyst performed a revenue analysis for each score band as in Exhibit 12-1. The total revenue is calculated as:

  *# Responders * Average $ balance transfer * (Fee% + APR%).*

Take the first score band 800+ for example, the total revenue =
  *40 * $1,000 * (3% + 3%) = $40,000 * 6% = $2,400.*

Exhibit 12-1 Revenue by Credit Bureau Score

Credit Bureau Score Range	# Accounts	# Reponse Rate	# Balance Transfer	$ Avg BT	Total $ Transferred	Fee %	APR	Total $ Revenue
800+	8,000	0.50%	40	$ 1,000	$ 40,000	3.00%	3.00%	$ 2,400
760-799	10,000	1.00%	100	$ 1,000	$ 100,000	3.00%	3.00%	$ 6,000
720-759	10,000	2.00%	200	$ 1,000	$ 200,000	3.00%	3.00%	$ 12,000
700-719	8,000	3.00%	240	$ 1,000	$ 240,000	3.00%	3.00%	$ 14,400
680-699	6,000	4.00%	240	$ 1,000	$ 240,000	3.00%	3.00%	$ 14,400
660-679	4,000	6.00%	240	$ 1,000	$ 240,000	3.00%	3.00%	$ 14,400
Total	46,000	2.30%	1,060		$ 1,060,000			$ 63,600

Next, the analyst calculated the total cost for each score band. The total cost consists of three main cost items, as shown in Exhibit 12-2:

▸ Dollar Credit Loss. The annualized dollar loss rate is measured from the actual performance of the previous campaign. Multiplying that by the total dollar balance transferred would provide the total dollar credit loss.

▸ Mailing Cost. Suppose the direct mail cost is $0.50 per letter. Multiplying the unit cost by the total number of prospect accounts in each score band would give you the total cost of the mailing.

▸ Cost of Fund. The card issuer is a full-service bank that enjoys the low cost of the fund from the deposit accounts. Multiplying the 25 basis point cost of the fund with the total dollar balance transferred would capture the cost of the fund.

Exhibit 12-2 Profitability Analysis by Credit Bureau Score

Credit Bureau Score Range	Annualized $ Loss Rate	Total $ Loss	Mailing Cost @ $.50	Cost of Fund @ 0.25%	Total Cost	Total $ Revenue	Total $ Profit
800+	0.50%	$ 200	$ 4,000	$ 100	$ 4,300	$ 2,400	$ (1,900)
760-799	1.00%	$ 1,000	$ 5,000	$ 250	$ 6,250	$ 6,000	$ (250)
720-759	2.00%	$ 4,000	$ 5,000	$ 500	$ 9,500	$ 12,000	$ 2,500
700-719	3.00%	$ 7,200	$ 4,000	$ 600	$ 11,800	$ 14,400	$ 2,600
680-699	4.00%	$ 9,600	$ 3,000	$ 600	$ 13,200	$ 14,400	$ 1,200
660-679	5.00%	$ 12,000	$ 2,000	$ 600	$ 14,600	$ 14,400	$ (200)
Total	3.21%	$ 34,000	$ 23,000	$ 2,650	$ 59,650	$ 63,600	$ 3,950

The analyst then subtracted the total cost from the total revenue to get the total dollar profit for each score band.

This profitability analysis revealed that only accounts in the middle score range, from 680 to 759, are expected to generate profit from the balance transfer campaign.

The bottom score band of 660–679 has most of the dollar loss, $12,000, among all score bands. That is due to the higher dollar loss rate as the score decreases. The $12,000 credit loss took away most of the revenue, thus making this segment slightly unprofitable with a loss of $200.

The top score band of 800+ only has an expected credit loss of $200. Why does it expect to have the largest total loss of $1,900?

This is because the response rate from the 800+ score band is very low, at only 0.5%. There are not many responders to the balance transfer offer, and thus the total expected revenue is only $2,400. The revenue is far less than the mailing cost of $4,000. Therefore, although the credit loss is very low, the response is too low to make this segment profitable.

A similar reason causes the 760-799 score band to be slightly unprofitable, with an expected loss of $250.

Based on this analysis, the risk analyst recommended targeting accounts with credit bureau scores from 660 to 759 only. In this score range, a total of 24,000 prospects are expected to generate $680,000 of balance and $6,300 of profit.

Further Opportunities

For the high score segments, especially the only slightly unprofitable 760–799 segment, response modeling can be used to identify prospects who are most likely to respond to the balance transfer offer. Better targeting could significantly lower the mailing cost and turn the high score segment into a profitable one.

For the low score 660–679 segment, credit loss is the largest cost item. Further risk segmentation might be able to carve out a sub-segment with lower risk and become profitable targets.

12.1.2 Decision Elements

Typical decision elements used in risk criteria for a balance transfer campaign include:

☑ Account Status Code

☑ Days Delinquent or Cycles Delinquent

☑ Credit Bureau Score — the latest refreshed score

☑ Behavior Score

☑ Month on Book

☑ Open to Buy — make sure there is enough room for a balance transfer

☑ External Credit Card Balance or Non-Mortgage Debt — only target those with enough external balance, otherwise it is a waste of direct mail costs

☑ Special Payment Plan Indicator

Additional decision elements such as *delinquency history in the last 24 months* or *current utilization* could be used to refine the risk criteria further. However, as these factors are usually encompassed in risk scores, any additional risk identification will probably be limited.

12.1.3 Measurement of Risk

If a card issuer has already recently rolled out multiple balance transfer campaigns, there is actual data to analyze the distribution of responders by risk band and their subsequent performances.

If an issuer does not have enough balance transfer campaigns to draw the experience yet, it would be safe to assume that the responders' risk profile skews a bit downward toward the lower end of each score band.

This is because those customers with lower scores tend to carry higher balances, thus have a bigger need to take advantage of the low APR offered by balance transfer.

During performance tracking, the actual risk metrics should be compared against the assumptions used in the business case to see how close they are. If off too much, you want to explore the reasons behind the gap and see how to fine-tune the assumptions for future campaigns so the estimate for the next campaign can be more accurate.

Finance Team

Ideally, the business case of a balance transfer campaign should be created by the finance team, which has a more intimate knowledge of the portfolio's profit and loss dynamics. They typically use cash flow analysis to calculate the net present value of the campaign, which would be more accurate than the quick analysis in Example 12.1.

However, finance is a very busy team. Not every lender can afford to have their finance team plugged into every credit campaign. As a matter of fact, most lenders probably don't do this, although I would advocate the close involvement of finance whenever possible.

In the absence of the close involvement of finance professionals, the project team should still do a quick analysis just to have an estimate of the campaign's profitability beforehand, in order to make sure the design of the campaign roughly meets the profitability objective.

Beyond Profitability

There are also times that the campaign profitability is not what the card issuer is after in the near term, or not the only thing that the issuer is after.

In a full-service bank, a balance transfer effectively engages the customer for an extended time such as 12 to 18 months. This is an excellent window of opportunity for the bank to cross-sell other banking products.

If the bank is able to get the card customer to bring their primary checking account over and becomes the customer's primary bank, not only can the bank earn revenue from the checking accounts, but it also has access to the deposit as a low-cost funding source and has the opportunity to cross-sell even more products, such as home lending and wealth management.

In this case, there is a strategic benefit to the bank in acquiring the transfer of the credit card's balance. Even though the P&L of a balance transfer campaign might barely break even by itself, the additional cross-selling opportunity can make it a huge win for the bank.

12.1.4 Variants of Balance Transfer

It is worth mentioning that the concept of balance transfer has evolved into some new products and services in the consumer lending industry over the years.

Debt Consolidation Loan

After the great financial crisis of 2008, various personal loan lenders emerged in order to satisfy the underserved loan demands from consumers and small businesses. Besides the smooth application and approval processes empowered by technology, one main incentive for consumers and small businesses to embrace the personal loan is the relatively lower interest rate compared to the traditional credit card.

Leveraging the low rate, the customers effectively consolidate their existing debts into a new personal loan and save financing costs.

Installment Loan on Credit Card

In the face of the balance attrition to personal loan and balance transfer offers from peers, some card issuers began to introduce new features to allow customers to pay selected purchases via installments, within the same credit card account.

The leaders of such innovations include Citibank and American Express in the U.S. and CIBC in Canada[1].

The beauty of this new feature is to allow the customer to enjoy the lower interest rate within an existing card account, saving the hassle of transferring a balance to another account. In addition, the customer has the flexibility to choose which transactions to put on an installment plan. The payments for both the regular card balance and the new installment loan are then managed within the same card account.

12.2 Interest Only

For revolving credit products such as credit card and line of credit, the monthly minimum required payment typically consists of a small portion of the principal balance plus all interest and fees.

One way to encourage the accountholder to keep more balance in the account is to ask the customer to pay only the interest and fee portion. As most customers would not incur any fee, such as a late fee or an NSF fee, the requested payment essentially is just the interest charge in the current period. Thus, this is called an "interest only" payment.

Because the principal portion is not required, the monthly minimum required payment would be significantly reduced. Let's look at such an example of a line of credit account in Example 12-2.

Example 12-2 Interest Only Significantly Reduces Monthly Payment

There is a line of credit account with a 5% annual interest rate. The average daily balance in the current billing cycle is $20,000. At the end of the billing cycle, the minimum payment due is calculated.

Under a regular payment method, assumed as 3% of balance plus interest charged in the current billing cycle, the minimum payment required is:

$20,000 x 3% + 20,000 x 5% /12 = $600 + $83.33 = $683.33.

With the interest only method, the minimum payment required is just the interest portion:

$$20,000 \times 5\% / 12 = \$83.33$$

The latter method would free up $600 cash outflow for the customer, which provides quite some flexibilities to the customer's personal finance.

In Example 11-2, the interest only method would reduce the monthly required payment by 88%, which is fairly significant. The sources of significance are: 1) a large existing balance, and thus a higher portion of the principal balance; 2) a low interest rate charged, and thus a low interest amount each month.

Thus, interest only is an effective tool to drive up the balance and engage customers of line of credit accounts, which typically have a large balance if utilized and a low interest rate.

For a line of credit, interest only can actually be applied to selected accounts on a permanent basis. However, the lender needs to do this very carefully — this should only be offered to customers with excellent credit. You do not want to provide this reduced payment option to someone who does not have the financial discipline to control debt growth and make timely monthly payments.

Of course, the lender always has the option to convert this interest only payment method back to a normal one whenever it is deemed necessary.

For a high interest rate product such as a credit card, it does not make sense to offer the interest only on a permanent basis. It should be used selectively only on a limited basis.

12.3 Skip a Payment

Similar to interest only, some card issuers resort to "skip-a-payment" campaigns to temporarily stop the minimum required payment for one month in order to generate more revenue.

By its name, a skip-a-payment campaign allows selected accounts to completely skip a payment for a month, effectively lowering the minimum required payment to zero.

For accounts that do take up this skip-a-payment offer and do not pay anything in the current month, as the balance is not paid off, the interest charge will continue to accrue.

While the cardholders do not need to pay anything in the current month, the total outstanding balance plus accrued interest charge are expected to be paid eventually. Actually, the payment is expected to resume in the following month, as it is only skip "a" payment.

The additional interest charge accrued on accounts that embraced the skip-a-payment offer Is the revenue growth that the lender is after by deploying such a campaign.

Again, it is important to only target the right customers with acceptable risk. There is no point in accruing interest on accounts that have a financial difficulty in paying it back.

For the credit bureau reporting, skip-a-payment will not be reported as a delinquency, thus there is no negative impact on the customer's credit score.

Some card issuers run this campaign once every 6 months, aiming to offer it to those customers who need a break after typical holiday spending. Used on the right customers, this is another good tactic to grow revenue.

12.4 Disaster Relief Measures

It should be pointed out that these portfolio stimulation tactics can also be used to serve customers as disaster relief measures, often with slight adaptions to the nature and severity of the disaster.

Balance transfer, interest only, and skip-a-payment: they are able to stimulate portfolio growth with a lower financial charge or temporally reduce the payment amount required. This is exactly what customers need when they are hit by a disaster.

From hurricanes and wildfires to the more recent COVID-19 pandemic, disasters always occur, if not more frequently than before.

For customers hit by these unfortunate events, lenders usually respond with various relief measures. This is what lenders should do — provide some financial relief to customers who are not at fault. These acts effectively buy some time for customers to regain their solid financial footings.

In 2020, all lenders in the U.S. and Canada provided various financial relief measures to their customers who were impacted by the COVID-19 pandemic[2,3]. Skip-a-payment or payment deferral for multiple months is the most common form. Canadian banks also lowered the APR on credit cards to around 10%. After a payment deferral period ends, some lenders also provide interest only payment options to customers.

At the end of the day, the lenders who are able to provide the services their customers need — to lower their financial burden and help them manage difficult times — will win the trust and lasting relationships with their clients.

RISK INFRASTRUCTURE

Chapter 13
Risk Data

Data is the foundation of all risk analysis. To make the analytical job more effective, it would be best for the risk team to have their own data mart, in which the data is organized in such a way that the risk insights can be extracted quickly.

In this chapter, Section 13.1 introduces a few common data structures of the risk data mart. Section 13.2 discusses how to ensure data quality by establishing a quality control process. Section 13.3 addresses data retention — how to store data for the long term.

13.1 Risk Data Mart

13.1.1 The Need for a Risk Data Mart

Risk-related data usually comes from various sources, such as the origination system, the account host system, risk decision engines, credit bureau files, the collections system, and offline campaign files.

As there are unique analytical methodologies, as well as frequent reporting needs, it would be best to have a dedicated risk data mart to support the risk analysis and reporting mandates.

For similar reasons, any sizable lender would have its own marketing data mart, finance data mart, etc., in order to satisfy the unique needs of each function.

13.1.2 Risk Data Structure

Denormalized

Because the main objective of a risk data mart is to support risk analysis and reporting, the data organization and data structure do not necessarily follow the principle of "normalization" for a data warehouse.

For example, the account balance is a frequently used field in various reports. Thus it might appear in multiple tables within a risk data mart. The duplication of one field would occupy more storage and resources. This is against the normalization principle of data warehouse design, where data redundancy is minimized. However, the "denormalized" data structure is very useful for making the end user's job as efficient as possible.

Data Elements

Depending on the source of data and whether any calculation is involved, there are various types of data elements that should be included in the risk data mart.

Raw Data

Some important data elements are straight copies of raw data from the system record, such as *income* from the origination system record, or *credit limit* from the account host system.

Label

Sometimes, a data element just has an alphanumeric value and has no meaning for those who don't know the underlying business meaning that each alphanumeric value is mapped to. In this case, it is best to create a derived variable to translate the raw value into a meaningful data label.

For example, one lender assigns the application from a branch with the value 1 in the *application channel* field. For an application from the Internet, the value 2 is assigned.

In order to facilitate understanding, it is best to create a new data field *"application channel name"* as the label for application channel, with values of "Branch" and "Internet" respectively.

Missing Value

Sometimes a data field has a value missing for some records in the raw file. This could create issues for the downstream data analysis, as some programming languages such as SAS might automatically exclude these records with a missing value.

Thus, the risk analyst has to create a step to manually convert any missing value to zero.

Since some of these fields, such as *balance* or *delinquency cycle* are commonly used, it is best to address this in the risk data mart by translating missing values to zeros for all numeric fields. This will save risk analysts' time and also reduce the possibility of errors in data analysis.

Variable Type Conversion

Sometimes, the raw value of a field comes in as a string. This happens in some risk strategy record files because the system populates zeros in front of the numeric values in order to keep the lengths of the field contents the same.

In this case, a risk analyst has to convert the string value to a numeric value each time, before performing any calculation.

If the numeric version of the data field is generated in the data mart, it would save the risk analysts from having to perform the data conversion steps.

Ratio

Some elements are calculated based on multiple raw data elements, such as *utilization* of a credit card account = *balance / credit limit*.

These commonly used ratio fields should be pre-calculated in the data mart.

Grouping

Some data elements are commonly used by grouping in risk reports, such as FICO. Thus, it is convenient to provide a common grouping as a data element in addition to the raw FICO score, such as *FICO Group* with the value as "Low <630", "Medium 630-699", and "High 700+". As sometimes an account's FICO could be missing, it is always good to have a "Missing" category as well.

Conditional Calculation

Some data elements are derived but conditional on certain criteria. For example, $90+ days delinquent day is one of the common risk metrics. The calculation method is:

The value is equal to the current balance if the number of days delinquent is 90+ and is not a charge-off; otherwise, the value is 0.

Handling of a Special Value

For example, some credit bureau attributes have the value 999999999 populated when there is no relevant tradeline record available. In this case, the value of 999999999 should be converted to a value of 0 before any calculation is performed.

There is no limitation to the scenarios where derived variables are needed. Think of what you need and be creative.

After the initial data mart has been established, the risk team can always request additional data fields to be added later, if analytics show that these are useful for analytics, modeling, or reporting purposes.

Next, let's look at a couple of data structure examples for a revolving credit product.

Data Structure Example 1, Revolving Credit, Consolidated

Many raw data files are snapshots of individual accounts on a given date. Examples include the account master file and the account statement file.

Take the account master file at the end of each month as an example, which is often used in monthly reporting. The individual records come in as shown in Exhibit 13-1.

Exhibit 13-1 Sample Records in the Monthly File

January month-end file

Account Number	Balance
1001	$ 101.00
1002	$ 102.00
1003	$ 103.00

Feburary month-end file

Account Number	Balance
1001	$ 201.00
1002	$ 202.00
1003	$ 203.00

March month-end file

Account Number	Balance
1001	$ 301.00
1002	$ 302.00
1003	$ 303.00

Because some analyses, such as a year-over-year analysis, require 13–24 months of data, one way to organize the performance data is to simply stack each monthly snapshot together in one big data table or dataset, as shown in Exhibit 13-2.

Exhibit 13-2 Consolidated Table with Records from Multiple Monthly Files

Account Number	Date	Balance
1001	31/01/2020	$ 101.00
1001	29/02/2020	$ 201.00
1001	31/03/2020	$ 301.00
...	...	...
1001	31/12/2020	$ 1,201.00
1002	31/01/2020	$ 102.00
1002	29/02/2020	$ 202.00
1002	31/03/2020	$ 302.00
...	...	...
1002	31/12/2020	$ 1,202.00
1003	31/01/2020	$ 103.00
1003	29/02/2020	$ 203.00
1003	31/03/2020	$ 303.00
...	...	...
1003	31/12/2020	$ 1,203.00

As some revolving credit products could have really long tenure, a decision needs to be made regarding how many months of data are retained in this big table. Typically, 24 months or 36 months are enough to allow year-over-year analysis, although the table does not have to stop there if storage and performance are not issues.

Origination Data

Sometimes, origination information is required for reporting and analytical purposes.

An individual application table usually exists with records from the origination system, which houses all the key risk information, such as credit bureau score, income, debt-to-income ratio, application date, decision date, and the final approval or decline decision.

For approved applications, there is an account number by way of which you can link to the performance table. You can actually skip the step of joining the application table with the performance table by creating a new table with the key application data fields appended to the consolidated performance table, as in Exhibit 13-3.

Exhibit 13-3 Consolidated Table with Origination Data Appended

Account Number	Date	Origination FICO	Origination Income	...	Origination Limit	Balance	Limit	...	Cycle Delinquency
1001	31/01/2020	720	$ 80,000	...	$ 10,000	$ 101.00	$ 10,000		0
1001	29/02/2020	720	$ 80,000		$ 10,000	$ 201.00	$ 10,000		0
1001	31/03/2020	720	$ 80,000		$ 10,000	$ 301.00	$ 10,000		1
...			...		...		...		...
1001	31/12/2020	720	$ 80,000		$ 10,000	$ 1,201.00	$ 10,000		0
1002	31/01/2020	660	$ 70,000		$ 5,000	$ 102.00	$ 5,000		0
1002	29/02/2020	660	$ 70,000		$ 5,000	$ 202.00	$ 5,000		1
1002	31/03/2020	660	$ 70,000		$ 5,000	$ 302.00	$ 5,000		0
...			...		...		...		...
1002	31/12/2020	660	$ 70,000		$ 5,000	$ 1,202.00	$ 5,000		0
1003	31/01/2020	750	$ 100,000		$ 12,000	$ 103.00	$ 15,000		0
1003	29/02/2020	750	$ 100,000		$ 12,000	$ 203.00	$ 15,000		0
1003	31/03/2020	750	$ 100,000		$ 12,000	$ 303.00	$ 15,000		0
...			...		...		...		...
1003	31/12/2020	750	$ 100,000		$ 12,000	$ 1,203.00	$ 15,000		0

Data Structure Example 2, Revolving Credit, Consolidated and Transposed

Another way to organize the revolving credit data is to transpose the 24 monthly records for one account into one long record, with the key metric from each month as a field, as shown in Exhibit 13-4.

Exhibit 13-4 Consolidated and Transposed Monthly Data

Account Number	Date	Balance1	Balance2	Balance3	...	Balance24	Avg. Bal. Last 3M	Avg. Bal. Last 6M	Avg. Bal. Last 12M
2001	31/12/2020	$ 2,001.00	$ 2,002.00	$ 2,003.00		$ 2,024.00	$ 2,023.00	$ 2,021.50	$ 2,012.50
3001	31/12/2020	$ 3,001.00	$ 3,002.00	$ 3,003.00		$ 3,024.00	$ 3,023.00	$ 3,021.50	$ 3,012.50
4001	31/12/2020	$ 4,001.00	$ 4,002.00	$ 4,003.00		$ 4,024.00	$ 4,023.00	$ 4,021.50	$ 4,012.50

In this way, the transpose step can be skipped when you want to compare a metric such as the balance from one point of time to another, which is often needed to show the trending over multiple months. It is also easy to create some derived momentum metrics, such as score change or balance change in a given period.

Data Dictionary

It is important to have a good data dictionary to specify what Balance 1, Balance 2, etc. are referring to.

In Exhibit 13-4, balance 1 refers to the monthly balance 24 months ago. Since the table creation date is December 31, 2020, Balance 1 refers to the balance on January 1st, 2019, Balance 2 refers to the balance on February 28, 2019, and so on. Balance

24 is the balance on the table creation date of December 31, 2020.

Average Balance in Last 3 Months is based on the 3 most recent months, which are October, November and December 2020.

Average Balance in Last 6 Months is based on the 6 most recent months, which are from July 2020 to December 2020.

Average Balance in Last 12 Months is based on the most recent 12 months, which are from January 2020 to December 2020.

Once users are familiar with the definition of these fields, they can easily create various reports and perform diverse analyses without spending too much time on data manipulation.

One thing to note is that, if there are too many variables you want to include as transposed ones, the 24 monthly occurrences could add up quickly. As a result, the data mart could become large, especially for a large portfolio. The storage and performance issues need to be considered as well.

After reviewing the data structure for revolving credit products, let's look at similar data structures for installment loans.

Data Structure Example 3, Installment Loan, Consolidated

For installment loans, each loan has a fixed term. Most analysis of installment loans is based on origination vintage, where loans with the same tenure are often measured and compared.

Thus, it would be convenient to include the monthly data with the account tenure (month-on-book as of loan creation date) already calculated.

In Exhibit 13-5, 3 loans were opened in the month of January, February, and March, respectively. They start with the same $1,200 balance and will pay down $100 each month.

Exhibit 13-5 Example of Month-end File for Installment Loan

January month-end file

Account Number	Open Date	Balance
6001	15-Jan-20	$ 1,200.00

Feburary month-end file

Account Number	Open Date	Balance
6001	15-Jan-20	$ 1,100.00
6002	08-Feb-20	$ 1,200.00

March month-end file

Account Number	Open Date	Balance
6001	15-Jan-20	$ 1,000.00
6002	08-Feb-20	$ 1,100.00
6003	20-Mar-20	$ 1,200.00

When these monthly records are stacked together with calculated month-on-book, the consolidated file will look like the table in Exhibit 13-6:

Exhibit 13-6 Consolidated Monthly Records for Installment Loans

Account Number	Date	Open Date	Months on Book	Balance
6001	31/01/2020	15-Jan-20	1	$ 1,200.00
6001	29/02/2020	15-Jan-20	2	$ 1,100.00
6001	31/03/2020	15-Jan-20	3	$ 1,000.00
...	...	...	...	...
6001	31/12/2020	15-Jan-20	12	$ 100.00
6002	29/02/2020	08-Feb-20	1	$ 1,200.00
6002	31/03/2020	08-Feb-20	2	$ 1,100.00
...	...	...	...	...
6002	31/12/2020	08-Feb-20	11	$ 200.00
6003	31/03/2020	20-Mar-20	1	$ 1,200.00
6003	30/04/2020	20-Mar-20	2	$ 1,100.00
...	...	...	...	...
6003	31/12/2020	20-Mar-20	10	$ 300.00

Similar to Example 1 for revolving credit, you can also append origination information in the data so it is easier to analyze the performance by key origination metric, as shown in Exhibit 13-7.

Exhibit 13-7 Consolidated with Origination Data, Installment Loan

				Orignation Data Fields				Performance Data Fields	
Account Number	Date	Open Date	Months on Book	Origination FICO	Origination Income	...	Balance	Cycle Delinquency	...
6001	31/01/2020	15-Jan-20	1	720	$ 80,000		$ 1,200.00	0	
6001	29/02/2020	15-Jan-20	2	720	$ 80,000		$ 1,100.00	0	
6001	31/03/2020	15-Jan-20	3	720	$ 80,000		$ 1,000.00	1	
...	...	...	...	...	...		...	...	
6001	31/12/2020	15-Jan-20	12	720	$ 80,000		$ 100.00	0	
6002	29/02/2020	08-Feb-20	1	660	$ 70,000		$ 1,200.00	1	
6002	31/03/2020	08-Feb-20	2	660	$ 70,000		$ 1,100.00	0	
...	...	...	...	...	...		...	...	
6002	31/12/2020	08-Feb-20	11	660	$ 70,000		$ 200.00	0	
6003	31/03/2020	20-Mar-20	1	750	$ 100,000		$ 1,200.00	0	
6003	30/04/2020	20-Mar-20	2	750	$ 100,000		$ 1,100.00	0	
...	...	...	...	...	...		...	...	
6003	31/12/2020	20-Mar-20	10	750	$ 100,000		$ 300.00	0	

Data Structure Example 4, Installment Loan, Consolidated and Transposed

As vintage analysis is the most common methodology for installment loan risk analytics, it would be easier for the user to access a table with the monthly installment loan data all transposed into one long record, as in Example 2, for revolving credit.

Exhibit 13-8 shows the transposed table for the same three sample accounts in Exhibit 13-6.

Exhibit 13-8 Consolidated and Transposed Monthly Data for Installment Loan

Account Number	Date	Open Date	Balance1	Balance2	Balance3	...	Balance10	Balance11	Balance12
2001	31/12/2020	15-Jan-20	$ 1,200.00	$ 1,100.00	$ 1,000.00		$ 300.00	$ 200.00	$ 100.00
3001	31/12/2020	08-Feb-20	$ 1,200.00	$ 1,100.00	$ 1,000.00		$ 300.00	$ 200.00	
4001	31/12/2020	20-Mar-20	$ 1,200.00	$ 1,100.00	$ 1,000.00		$ 300.00		

As in Example 2, a well-documented data dictionary is important. Here Balance1 means the balance when an account is at month-on-book 1, the first month on book. Balance 2 means the balance when an account reaches month-on-book 2, and so on.

With this transposed data structure, it is fairly easy to create various vintage reports and compare loans that have the same tenure.

13.2 Data Quality

Data quality is paramount for risk analysis or any data analysis. Poor data will lead to poor analysis and poor decisions.

Here are some recommended practices that can help you ensure risk data of good quality.

Testing at Launch

When developing a data mart, all straight copies and derived variables need to go through testing in order to make sure the ETL (Extract, Transform, and Load) process is executed as per design. Representatives from the risk team should be part of the testing exercise to make sure the data output is exactly what is expected.

After initial development, the ETL process will continue to run with the frequency designed, such as daily, weekly, or monthly. However, it cannot be assumed that the data mart will always run without error.

Ongoing Monitoring

Although we would all like to have the data mart and related data feeds running smoothly, in reality, there is a real possibility that a fully tested and smoothly running process will break down at some point. Thus, ongoing monitoring as a quality control measure is also needed.

Ideally, each data element in the data mart should be monitored, and the monitoring job should also be automated.

The data quality check rule should be designed based on the characteristic of each variable. Some examples of data quality rules are:

- ☑ Average value of loan balance changes should be within 10%.
- ☑ Maximum value of a credit card limit is within $50,000.
- ☑ The date of the credit bureau score should change every month, as the score gets refreshed monthly.

Ideally, the breaking of such rules should automatically trigger an alert to the risk teams and relevant stakeholders, so an investigation can be conducted to find the root cause and take corrective action.

13.3 Data Archive

A data mart typically stores the commonly used data elements. There will be times that the new addition of data elements is needed, so the original system files need to be retained.

Actually, for smaller financial institutions that are just starting a lending business line or lack the budget to develop a risk data mart as of yet, the original system files are the only data sources.

In any case, all of the system's raw files need to be retained as the sources of original data. These files — especially the daily files — could accumulate quickly and take up the storage space.

Thus, at some point, the old data needs to be removed in order to make space for new data. Generally, the retention of risk data should follow the lender's overall data retention policy.

However, in practice, due to the limited space, not all data within a bank's data retention policy is able to be retained online. "Online" means the files are kept on a server so that the risk team can use a data query tool to directly access the data whenever needed, in the same way as the most recent data files.

If data files are moved "offline," they do not disappear; instead, they are copied in a data storage device such as a data tape. You can still access the data needed by submitting a request. Then the information technology team will need to physically locate the data tape and load the data back online, which is obviously a bit of a hassle, but still doable.

Because of the hassle and the time it takes to bring the archived data back online, the risk team will probably want to negotiate that the data stays online as long as possible. Of course, the objective is not necessarily to retain everything online forever, but at least those that you frequently need should stay online and be available at any time.

Exhibit 13-9 shows an example of a policy for credit card risk data retention, which aims to provide adequate data to cover most needs.

Exhibit 13-9 A Data Retention Policy Example

Files	Online Retention Time
Monthly Portfolio Snapshot Files	5 years
Strategy Log Files (decision elements and actions) - Origination - Authorization (credit risk portion) - Credit Line - Collections - etc.	**5 years** - For some credit decisions, you want to see the long-term performance over 24 months.
Daily Files - Authorization (all types of authorization) - Payment	**2 years** - Needed for year-over-year analysis; - Some credit portfolios have strong seasonality.

Chapter 14
Risk System

14.1 Risk System Overview

Multiple risk systems are involved throughout a credit product's credlt life cycle. Here is an introduction to some that are more commonly used.

Account Origination Decision System

When a credit application comes in, there is an account origination decision system to implement the credit decision strategy and limit/loan strategy.

For applications requiring further review for reasons of risk or fraud, the system is also able to route the applications to various queues. These pending applications will be reviewed by the underwriting or the fraud team, as assigned.

Examples of account origination decision systems include Capstone, Strategy Manager/System Builder, and Zoot. These different systems have different interfaces but similar functions.

As with any decision system, an origination decision system is usually able to support multiple strategies being run in parallel in a champion/ challenger framework.

Account Hosting System

Once an account is approved in the origination decision system, basic information, such as customer name, address, credit limit, or loan amount, is sent to the account hosting system to establish the account.

This account hosting system keeps the record for the account. All financial transactions of purchase, payment, interest, and fee accrual will be recorded here.

Examples of account hosting systems include FDR, TSYS, and Vision.

Account Management Decision System

For a revolving credit product like credit cards, there are many decision points after an account is opened. Here the account management decision system refers to the system consisting of a set of modules to enable decisions in specific areas, which include authorizations, credit line management, collections, reissue, etc.

Examples of account management decision systems include TRIAD, ACS, and Strategy Manager/System Builder. These decision systems can implement decision tree based strategies with the champion/challenger design.

With each particular transaction or event, the transaction or account will enter a particular module in the account management decision system.

Authorization

For example, an authorization goes through the authorization module. During the authorization process, several components will actually be involved — credit policy, fraud strategy, and credit risk authorization strategy. We have provided a more detailed introduction of authorization in Chapter 7.

Payment

When a payment comes in, there is a risk of the payment being returned later for various reasons. Thus, the lender can use a decision module designed specifically for payments to decide whether to hold the open-to-buy or even block the accounts associated with high-risk behaviors.

At Cycle Time

When an account cycles, right before the monthly statement is generated, it goes through a credit line management module to see if the credit line deserves to be increased or decreased.

If an account is delinquent at cycle time, it will also go through a delinquency collections module to see what kinds of collection actions should be assigned.

Reissue

About two months before the expiration date of the credit card plastic, depending on the settings that a card issuer chooses, the account will go through the reissue module to see if it still qualifies to receive a new plastic, and if so, how long the new valid period should be for the new plastic.

Collections System

When the collections strategy module within an account management decision system runs every day and creates a list of accounts for collections operations, this list will be uploaded into the collections system.

With the output from collections strategies, the accounts are sent to different queues.

Those eligible to receive a phone call will be loaded into a dialer that automatically dials the accounts' phone numbers for collectors. A collections manager can put further rules into the dialer system to determine which accounts get called first and how often.

Accounts that no longer have a valid phone number can be sent to a skip tracing queue, so collectors with special knowledge can work on them.

Late stage delinquent accounts are usually sent to a dedicated collection team to collect on them manually.

With all kinds of collection activities happening, the collections system produces valuable data, such as which accounts were contacted, via which method, at what time, whether the customer was reached, if any promise-to-pay was made, and whether the promise-to-pay was kept. Such information can provide further feedback for the collection strategy to enhance the segmentation and risk assessment.

Fraud Decision and Queueing System

The fraud strategies at origination are usually part of the account origination decision system.

For transactional fraud management, there is usually a unique decision system deployed as part of the overall authorization process. This decision system can provide great flexibility for managing decline or queueing rules corresponding to various fraud schemes.

14.2 Implementation

The implementation of strategies in these decision systems is similar to a light version of code release in a software company, and the process thus closely resembles the software development life cycle to a certain degree.

Before the strategy is implemented, there is a strategy development step conducted by a risk analyst or consultant. Afterwards, the implementation would typically go through several major steps, as follows.

Requirement

After a new strategy is developed and gets approved by the management with proper authority, the strategy requirement is submitted to the credit system team. The requirements need to be properly documented.

The specific form of documentation often varies in different institutions. It could be a simple Word or Excel file. Regardless of the form used, it should state an overview of the changes, which products the changes are intended to apply to, who submits the changes, who approves them, intended implementation date, and detailed changes requested.

It is recommended that the requestor always has a review meeting with the credit system team in order to make sure the requirements are fully documented and clearly understood.

Analysis

After the requirement document is submitted, the credit system team reviews and analyzes the detailed requirements, to determine how to best accommodate the changes.

For most standard changes, such as score cut-offs, there should not be any issue.

In some cases, the requested changes cannot be accommodated with the system's existing functionality. The credit system team would then go back to the requestor to discuss alternative plans — maybe to change the requirement somewhat but to still achieve the same objectives, or to submit a custom request to the system vendor.

The custom request could take some time, as the vendor needs to go through its own project management process to manage the request.

Coding

Once having a design to satisfy the requirements, the credit system team starts to code the changes into the system. The coding always takes place in the test region first, so testing can be performed to ensure the requirement is coded correctly.

Testing

Testing is a crucial step, as proper testing can capture any mistake before the changes are released into production.

After the changes are coded into the test region, the credit system team should perform some basic testing to make sure the changes are working as intended.

To prepare the testing, appropriate test cases need to be created to represent the specific scenario to be tested. This might involve steps such as manually updating credit bureau scores, and posting multiple purchases and payments on the accounts, which could take multiple days.

If the testing fails for certain scenarios, the credit system team needs to research why that happened, figure out a solution, code new changes, and test again.

Some decision systems also provide strategy simulation capability so a new strategy can run against a sample of recent production data. Such a function should be utilized as additional testing in order to verify that the changes are performing as expected.

If all test cases have passed, the changes can be scheduled to release into the production environment.

Release

Once the changes are ready to move into the production environment, a release date is determined.

The release date is best set during weekdays, so that post production validation can be performed right away or on the next day.

I would recommend selecting the product release date on a Monday, Tuesday, or Wednesday night. This way, if something happens, you still have resources available to debug and fix it during the remaining weekdays. The last thing you want is to have to scramble to find people to deal with system outages over the weekend.

Production Validation

After the changes are released into production, both the credit system and credit risk teams need to monitor the transactions in production closely — using the earliest available data to confirm that the changes were implemented as intended and no other aspects are impacted unintentionally.

Proactive production validation will help detect issues early on, if there are any. Timely remediation will minimize losses or interruptions caused by unintended errors.

14.3 Systematic vs. Batch

Ideally, all risk strategies should be automated in credit systems, so decisions are automatically carried out based on the most up-to-date information.

In reality, however, for various reasons, there are also cases in which risk strategies are implemented via a batch process.

Systematic Approach

A systematic strategy with full automation is the best option for unsecured lending risk strategies, with a prerequisite that all underlying decision elements are already available in the credit system. In addition, the best scenario for the systematic approach is when the strategy design has been fully reviewed and approved and there is no plan to redesign the strategy in the short term, such as in 3–6 months.

Once fully tested, launched and subject to proper production validation, a strategy can be left running. The operational risk of the strategy not working is fairly low. Of course, some basic strategy monitoring should still take place, as nothing is completely without risk.

Batch Approach

A batch process usually involves more human involvement. First, there is one person who needs to execute the strategy offline (outside the credit system) and produce a file containing the risk decisions. Then another person in the credit system team who has privileged access will upload the decision file into the relevant system to drive the action.

As you can imagine, the human involvement could experience a breakdown of the process when there is staff turnover or a human error when executing the jobs.

Why does such an approach with higher operational risk get used sometimes?

This could be due to the fact that the current credit decision system does not have all the required decision elements available or the system implementation is too complicated. But the solution for either case leads to an extended project timeline.

In the meantime, there is a real desire to implement the new strategy quickly in order to reap benefits for the company right away. In this case, a batch process can help achieve quick delivery.

Another scenario is that the launch strategy is just meant as a pilot program. Thus, there is a good possibility that some changes in decision logic will occur after the result of the pilot program is available. Also, there is the possibility that the full program may not be implemented at all if the pilot program is unsuccessful.

Due to these uncertainties, there is no need to jump through hoops to go through the entire process needed to implement the pilot systematically.

It should be pointed out that, even for the batch process, there should still be a tester who can perform an independent validation in order to make sure the batch program correctly executes the strategy design. The whole "testing, implementation, and production testing" process should still be followed.

14.4 New Decision Elements

With the evolvement of business and ongoing analytics, there are often times that new decision elements need to be introduced in order to improve the effectiveness of risk strategies.

Placeholder Fields

Having anticipated the needs of new decision elements from various lenders, the account host system and risk strategy vendors usually reserve some placeholder fields for this purpose.

These placeholder fields have generic names such as *user defined field 1, user defined field 2*, etc.

For lenders, it is a good practice to assign one owner to manage the use of all the risk decision elements, especially in a large organization where there could be multiple risk teams using the same set of decision elements.

The risk decision element owner should maintain good documentation of which user-defined field has already been taken, what the meaning of the field in use is, which process is updating the field, at what frequency, in which decision strategy the field is being used, and who the contact person is if there is an issue with the data update.

Newly Developed Decision Elements

Sometimes there is a need to develop a brand new decision element. This is often the case if the new decision element will be used in real-time strategies, such as authorization and payment strategies, where a batch update process will not work.

Developing new decision elements would involve the credit system vendor, so there would be a price tag for the lender.

Also, it takes time to get on the credit system vendor's development and release schedule.

A good practice is for the lender to have a regular schedule with the credit system vendor, to thereby allow the introduction of new decision elements once a year, for example. This way, the requirements can be collected throughout the year. It would also be more economical to request multiple new decision element requests at once, as there is often a minimum overhead charge.

The approach of a regular schedule essentially asks the vendor to reserve resources every year in advance. If there is not enough work for this year, just advise the vendor in advance, and then the reserved resources can be released to other projects.

14.5 Test Case Management

To support the ongoing strategy changes and implementation, it is important for the lender to have a set of test applications and accounts ready to use at any time.

Test Region

With properly prepared test applications and test accounts, a lender can test the new risk strategies in the test region first. This provides an opportunity for the lender to review the changes against the requirements.

If any issue arises, there is no negative impact to the production environment. The credit system team just needs to make any necessary fix and then test again until the testing result is satisfactory.

Test Cases

In order to test the newly developed or modified strategies effectively, a variety of test cases are needed. Here, the test case refers to a particular scenario. For example, a test case for account origination could be an application that has a charge-off record within the last 12 months. A test case for account management could be an account with a FICO score of 680 and an existing limit of $5,000.

Test cases with credit bureaus

For application test cases, a lender needs to work with its credit bureau vendor to generate those test cases into the credit bureau's test regions. If the lender has a secondary credit bureau, the same test cases should be prepared in the secondary bureau's test region as well.

Test cases with an account host system

For test cases of an existing account, the lender can usually copy a sample of accounts from the production region into the test region. However, to get the specific test case or test scenario, the lender still needs to perform proper account maintenance activities, such as posting authorizations and payments, change credit limits, and update credit scores — this is called "account conditioning."

Annual test case refresh

One thing worth noting is that the test region usually gets refreshed once a year. With the refresh, all test cases and test strategies will be deleted.

Thus, it is important to plan out your testing activities. Make sure the needed testing activities are completed and test strategies are moved into production before the test region refresh date.

14.6 Credit System Management Staffing

Dedicated Risk System Team

With a large lender, there are usually multiple credit portfolios that require frequent strategy changes. The size of the lender can easily justify an internal team dedicated to credit system management.

This team will possess the knowledge of all risk systems used from origination to account management. They can also manage the test cases and conditioning to ensure that proper testing is in place before each production release.

Strategy and System Team in One

A small lender might not have the budget to retain a dedicated credit system team. Often, the responsibility of risk systems is also part of the risk strategy team's responsibilities.

The good thing about this arrangement is that, by knowing how the risk system works, the risk strategy developer can design the most effective strategy within the current system's capability.

Otherwise, the following scenario could happen — the strategy developer comes up with a new strategy on paper, but it requires that new decision elements or new system functionality be developed. This would result in significant time required to build the new strategy, which diminishes its potential benefit.

The downside of the strategy-and-system-team-in-one arrangement is that the risk strategy developer usually does not have formal training in system management. Thus, the team might not have all the necessary skills and mindset to conduct robust testing and deal with potential system issues.

Outsourcing

Another possible scenario is that a small lender might not have any in-house system expertise. In this case, it can actually choose to outsource the risk system management work to the decision system vendor.

In this way, there is no need for internal staff to go through the learning curve, as the system provider possesses a great amount of knowledge about its own system.

It is just a way to reallocate the resources of system management to the external vendor, which may not necessarily increase the lender's cost.

There are pros and cons associated with each of the above staffing approaches. At the end of the day, it is a balanced decision based on financial cost, internal expertise, and speed of implementation.

Chapter 15
Fraud

Fraud is a special discipline, and the breadth of this topic probably merits its own book. In practice, some fraud strategies intertwine with credit risk strategies. Thus, it is always good for credit risk professionals to understand, even at a high level, how fraud strategies work, even there is a separate dedicated Fraud team in your financial institution.

Also, at small financial institutions, some risk managers take on the responsibility of fraud management as well. That is actually how I got my experience in fraud at the beginning of my career.

This chapter is not only for risk professionals who might need to take on some fraud responsibilities. Even for people not directly involved with fraud, as long as you work in consumer credit industry, it is helpful to have a basic understanding of the main fraud controls.

Section 15.1 introduces typical fraud controls at account origination. Sections 15.2–15.4 address further fraud mitigation tactics for revolving credit products such as credit cards. Section 15.5 introduces various fraud systems and Section 15.6 covers the fraud strategy measurement.

15.1 Origination Fraud Controls

Fraud strategy is one of the main components of the origination strategy. Various tools are available from different vendors in this space, especially as the digital application becomes more prevalent in recent years.

A lender would typically deploy several standard tools to build the basic defense at account origination against the fraudsters, which will be covered in individual sections in this chapter:

☑ Fraud Alert from Credit Bureau

☑ Application Fraud Score

☑ Digital Fraud Mitigation Tool

☑ Out-of-wallet Questions

☑ Internal Fraud Database

15.1.1 Fraud Alert from Credit Bureau

The credit bureau receives account status reports from various lenders. If a credit account is reported as being fraudulent, the credit bureau will take note.

When an application inquiry comes in, the credit bureau will scan its database to locate the applicant. If one of the key items on the application is associated with reported fraud activities, an alert will be sent back to the lender along with the credit report and other credit attributes.

An example of such an alert would be a misused phone number, or a misused address.

With this alert, some lenders might just decline the applications while others could refer such applications to a special queue so the underwriter can work on them manually. The manual review might lead to a request for additional documents in order to authenticate the applicant.

15.1.2 Application Fraud Score

There are various vendors that can produce a fraud score for each credit application. The score assesses how likely it is that an application is fraudulent.

If the fraud risk represented by the fraud score is too high, the application should be declined immediately. Some analysis using either internal application data or comparable data from the vendor should help find the appropriate score cut-off point.

For applications above the minimum fraud score cut-off point, a lender can further segment them into low fraud score vs. high fraud score populations. Similar to credit scores, a high fraud score usually represents a lower fraud risk.

Even though these applications above the minimum fraud score cut-off will get approved, a lender can choose to assign a lower credit limit to a low fraud score population as a way to limit the initial credit exposure.

15.1.3 Digital Fraud Mitigation Tool

As more and more applications originate from laptops, smartphones, and mobile devices, so is the fraud associated with digital applications.

To address the issue in the increasingly important digital channel, multiple vendors have emerged who specialize in assessing the fraud risk of digital applications. The assessment is typically based on a combination of digital device information, behavior pattern, and application information.

For the sake of convenience, the output of the fraud risk assessment often comes as a fraud risk score. At the same time, some vendors also offer flexibility, so a lender can adjust the underlying rules and associated weights that produce the final score.

15.1.4 Out-of-Wallet Questions

For Internet applications or phone in applications, the lender can usually deploy a set of out-of-wallet questions to further identify the applicant to make sure they are truly the consumer that they claim to be.

Out-of-wallet questions, also known as knowledge-based questions, are often based on the consumer's credit bureau file. As many questions are related to the credit history, they cannot be answered even if you have access to the customer's wallet and all the identification documents inside — hence the name "out of wallet."

Some sample questions are:

☑ Which address did you live at previously?

☑ Did you ever have a car loan with bank A?

☑ Do you have a credit card with bank B?

The lender can choose which questions to ask from a list of questions predefined by the credit bureau vendor. The lender can also decide how many questions to use for an application and how many answers the applicant has to answer correctly in order to pass.

For example, one lender decides to use 4 questions from a predefined list and the applicant has to answer 3 of them correctly in order for the application to continue.

Note that the power of out-of-wallet questions is waning in recent years, as more and more data breaches have exposed the out-of-wallet data for fraudulent use.

15.1.5 Internal Fraud Database

A lender often maintains an internal database to include all identified fraudulent accounts. An application can be compared to these known fraud records to see if there is any match. The application with a match will usually be declined.

One dimension of the records is the zip code or postal code of the address. A lender can identify which geographic areas post a high fraud risk. If the risk is too high, these "hot zones" can be avoided altogether in a solicitation campaign. Alternately, special logic can be introduced to the applications from these hot zones to increase the decline rate and reduce the limit that is assigned, or refer the applications to a special queue for manual review.

15.2 Card Activation

Once a cardholder receives the new credit card (the actual plastic) in the mail, they can find a sticker on the plastic with instructions on how to activate the card. Once the customer inputs the required information via phone call or online and passes the activation check, the card issuer will know that the plastic is in the right hands and then flip an activation flag on in the system. The card is now activated and can be used to make purchases.

Nowadays, card issuers allow activation from either phone calls or over the Internet. Typically, the cardholder is asked to input the full digits of the card number, the card verification value or CVV (3 digits on the back of a VISA/MasterCard or 4 digits on the front of an American Express card), date of birth, and the last 4 digits of their Social Security number (SSN).

The card number and CVV checks ensure that the legitimate plastic is in the hands of the person who is attempting to activate it.

The date of birth and SSN checks aim to ensure that the person who is attempting to activate the card is the true cardholder.

For phone in activation, the IVR (interactive voice response) system can also check the phone number the individual is calling from against the phone number submitted during the application. If it does not match, the activation call could be routed to a live agent for further verification.

Card activation also applies if the customer receives a new plastic from an existing account, such as when an authorized user is added or a new plastic is issued after the old plastic is reported as lost or stolen.

Note that some card issuers are starting to move away from card activation and replace it with improved fraud detection strategies at transaction level.

15.3 Transactional Fraud

For credit cards, which could be used with a high frequency of purchases, the monitoring of daily transactions is an important part of fraud mitigation.

The transactional fraud rules, also called account management fraud rules, are implemented as part of the overall authorization process, attempting to stop the fraudulent activities during the transaction.

There is usually a transactional fraud score assigned for each authorization. This score is often provided by a vendor who specializes in transactional fraud scoring.

As the fraud risk levels associated with different scenarios vary, different score cut-offs are used with the various fraud rules.

Below are some typical transactional fraud rules and the fraud scenarios they are designed to address.

Excessive authorization

Too many transactions and large transaction values occur over a short span of time.

High risk transaction

Transactions with typical high risk merchandise, such as cash, gift cards, and electronics.

Account takeover

Changed purchase behavior after account profile change, such as address change, phone number change, or the addition of an authorized user.

Card not present

Transactions keyed in instead of swiped or read by chip readers. The risk of a card not present transaction is higher as there is a possibility that the card number has been stolen.

Online transaction

Internet transactions are inherently high risk, as it is easy for fraudsters to attempt these purchases from literally anywhere in the world with just a few keystrokes. Thus, there are often specialized rules for Internet transactions.

Out of region transaction

The transactions in a new region different from where the cardholder resides and typically transacts carry higher risk — especially if the geographic locations between adjacent transactions are too distant from each other, considering the normal transportation time required. An example would be transactions that took place in California and New York 5 minutes apart.

Out of country transaction

Similar to out of region transactions, out of country transactions also carry higher risk, as there are international fraud groups that specialize in compromising card information and then making large purchases on the other side of the globe. Hence, there are often specialized rules for out-of-country purchases.

To understand how transactional fraud rules work in conjunction with other controls during the authorization process, please refer to Section 7.1 Authorization Controls.

15.4 Payment Fraud

One common fraud scheme associated with credit card is *payment fraud*. Some people also refer to this scheme as *kiting* or a *bust-out*.

The way it works is that the accountholder maliciously makes a large payment to the account, but there are not enough funds to back the payment. An unsuspected card issuer would typically release the open-to-buy (available credit) right away, not knowing that the payment will eventually be returned.

As soon as the open-to-buy is available, the fraudster quickly maxes out the account's credit limit. Days later, the payment gets returned and the account is left with a large balance that is well over its credit limit.

Example 15-1 illustrates how a fraudster incurred a financial loss, doubling the credit limit of a credit card.

Example 15-1 Payment Fraud Loss Doubles the Credit Limit

> One credit card account has a $10,000 credit limit and currently has a $10,000 balance. The fraudster makes a $10,000 payment to the account. Treated as a normal account, the $10,000 open-to-buy is released right away and the balance is reduced to $0 overnight.
>
> The fraudster makes $10,000 in purchases within 2 days and brings the balance to the full limit of $10,000 again. On the third day, the $10,000 payment is returned as the banking account associated with the payment does not have the funds. The reversal payment is added onto the account and the balance then becomes $20,000.
>
> By taking advantage of the time that banks take to settle the payment, the fraudster effectively bypasses the credit limit and incurs a $20,000 loss on a $10,000 credit limit account.

Mitigation

By analyzing recent payment behavior relative to account balance and limit, the issuer is able to segment out payments with a high payment fraud risk.

For these payments, the issuer can choose to "float" the payment, i.e., to hold the open-to-buy for a number of days in case the payment might be returned. For very suspicious payments with the risk assessed as ultra-high, the account can even be temporarily blocked and routed to the fraud team for manual review.

15.5 Fraud Systems

Origination fraud strategy is usually coded in the same credit decision engine as the origination strategy.

For transactional fraud strategy, there is usually a fraud rule engine plugged into the card issuer processor's authorization process, so authorization can be declined as soon as risk is detected. The same system also has a queueing function, basically to put authorizations and accounts in various queues for the fraud team to manually review. Different queues could include approved authorizations or declined ones. Based on the review result, there might be further actions taken on the account, such as temporary blocking or closure.

Payment typically has another system to manage the float or no float decision, such as Payment Defender from the Fiserv/FDR.

15.6 Fraud Strategy Measurement

False Positive Rate

One key metric used to measure the effectiveness of a fraud strategy is the false positive rate, which is the ratio between the number of good cases (non-fraudulent ones) and the number of total cases identified by a given fraud strategy.

For example, one particular fraud decline rule declines 10 authorizations. Out of the 10 authorizations, two are subsequently confirmed as the truly fraudulent ones and the other 8 are deemed okay or non-fraudulent. In this case, then, the false positive rate is 8/10 = 80%.

An equivalent measure is the "good:bad ratio." In this case, it is 8 good authorizations to 2 bad ones = 4:1. This means that, under the particular fraud decline rule, for every 1 declined bad authorization, there are 4 good ones being declined as well.

Based on your particular credit portfolio's characteristics, such as product feature, P&L model, fraud operations staffing cost, a guideline of false positive rate or good:bad ratio can be established to guide the fraud decline and referral rules.

For example, one card portfolio determines that when the good:bad ratio is below 9:1, the lender definitely loses money if all the authorizations are approved. Thus, any fraud rule that can produce a good:bad ratio lower than 9:1, or a false positive rate less than or equal to 90%, should become a decline rule — the authorizations captured by these rules will be declined.

Similarly, the same lender might calculate that when the good:bad ratio is higher than 9:1 but lower than 25: 1, it is best to approve such authorizations, but also to put them in a queue for fraud operations to review them manually.

Overall, such authorizations are still profitable, so it justifies the approval; this way the customer experience of the majority of good accounts can be ensured. However, the fraud rate of these transactions is also high enough to warrant some manual detection and investigation work, so that the fraudulent cases could be identified to avoid further losses.

SECTION V
PORTFOLIO RISK MANAGEMENT

Chapter 16
Portfolio Risk Management

The previous chapters introduced different aspects of unsecured lending risk management. Think of them as different tools in your risk management toolkit — each can be used to achieve a specific portfolio management objective.

These different tools need to be deployed under the appropriate circumstances in order to help steer your portfolio towards the destination.

Beyond the tools, this chapter touches upon some portfolio risk management concepts at the overall portfolio level.

16.1 Portfolio Risk Appetite

Risk Appetite

First, it is important to set a portfolio risk appetite. There are many consumers and small businesses in the credit universe. Who are your target customers with the products and services you are offering? What is the accepted risk level for you to own the credit portfolio on the balance sheet and also to make a reasonable profit?

In the diverse consumer lending industry, there are many choices of customer segments for lenders to position their products and services. The risk appetite statement can help a lender set up a clear boundary within which to manage the portfolio risk.

Setting Risk Appetite

When setting the risk appetite of a particular credit portfolio, the overall profit model of the credit product, the credit characteristics of its main clientele, and overall company's risk appetite should be considered. A sub-prime loan portfolio would have a very different risk appetite from a premium credit card portfolio.

Some quantitative analysis is recommended to support the final risk appetite threshold versus other values.

The risk appetite statement should have a clear risk metric with a cap value, indicating the risk area that the portfolio should be operating within. Under the cap value, there is another lower threshold set as the alert level.

In Exhibit 16-1, a credit portfolio has a portfolio risk appetite of 8.0% net charge-off rate. The alert level is set at 6.0%.

Once the portfolio's net charge-off rate is above 6.0% and still below 8.0%, it is considered to have entered the yellow zone. Analysis and discussion should take place in order to perceive the reasons behind the loss rate increase and any possible actions to take in order to manage the portfolio risk within the 8.0% risk appetite that is established.

Exhibit 16-1 Example of a Portfolio's Risk Appetite

As all credit strategies' impacts on a portfolio tend to be long term, it is important to take mitigation actions while there is still a buffer, before the risk metric breaches the cap value. If you only act when the risk metric is over the cap, it is probably too late.

The risk appetite of a portfolio is usually reviewed annually, although it does not necessarily change every year.

Apply the Risk Appetite

The risk appetite metric will be an important part of the ongoing portfolio monitoring.

Equally important is to ensure that all credit decisions made in each decision area are aligned with the risk appetite.

What should be noted is that the particular threshold in each decision area might be different from the portfolio risk appetite threshold, depending on the particular decision area in the credit life cycle.

For example, new accounts tend to have a higher loss rate in the first 24 months compared to subsequent stages when accounts become more seasoned. It is normal to allow the new accounts cohort to have a peak loss rate of 10% in the first 24 months, for example, because analysis shows that the loss rate of the seasoned accounts, or those beyond 24 months, will have dropped to the green zone of less than 6%.

Feedback on Risk Appetite

Risk appetite is not set in stone. In practice, with first-hand experience from the field, the first-line risk and business teams can offer feedback on existing risk appetite and potentially influence the change.

Example 16.1 Expanded Risk Appetite Led to an Increase in Market Share

Exhibit 16-2 illustrates the profitability of lender A's credit card customers by credit bureau score. Lender A's old risk appetite only allowed itself to operate in the low risk zone, which left more profitable customers to competitors.

Facing the pressure of sliding market share, the business team and the risk team began the discussion to see how they could move down the risk curve into a 'sweeter' spot.

Exhibit 16-2 Illustrative Profitability and Loss Rate by FICO

With detailed analysis and multiple discussions among the stakeholders, the lender eventually decided to increase its portfolio risk appetite by 100 bps. This led to the expansion of multiple credit strategies, which helped the lender regain the market share by 150 bps 12 months later.

16.2 Portfolio-level Risk Management

For a risk professional, it is important to establish the portfolio view — understanding key levers available and how to effectively use them in conjunction to manage the credit portfolio and achieve objectives.

Even if you just start your career as an analyst, having a portfolio view will help you see how your work fits into the overall portfolio management framework. You will find your work more meaningful when you understand how it contributes to the profit and loss of the portfolio. It could also help you plan your next role in order to gain more portfolio management experience.

Next, let's look at a couple of typical exercises in portfolio risk management.

16.2.1 Risk Attribution

The risk team will often be asked to explain the changes of key portfolio-level risk metrics and attribute the changes to a few underlying factors. This exercise is called "risk attribution."

Risk attribution helps senior management understand the dynamics behind the change and also would help plan out subsequent actions.

Generally speaking, you can look at several areas in order to determine which major factors contribute to the latest portfolio risk changes. Typical factors include:

☑ an industry trend, often influenced by the particular phase in the current business cycle;

☑ a regional event, such as economic event or natural disaster;

☑ recent major portfolio initiatives, from both risk and business sides, such as a major acquisition campaign, a credit line increase campaign, a new collection strategy, or operational changes;

☑ changes of specific products or business segments.

Let's look at Example 16.2 to see how a portfolio risk attribution exercise reveals the underlying reasons of a rising risk level for a portfolio.

Example 16.2 Portfolio Risk Attribution Analysis

For example, a personal loan portfolio experienced significant increases of loss amount and loss rate this year vs. last year. The senior management team wanted to understand what had happened and what actions could be taken in order to manage the loss down.

The risk team thoroughly reviewed a list of potential contributing factors and summarized the findings in Exhibit 16-3.

Exhibit 16-3 An Example of Risk Attribution Analysis of Loss Rate

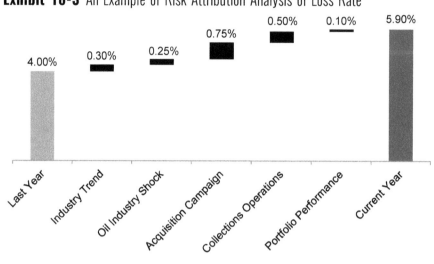

The attribution reveals that the largest contributing factor is the acquisition campaign conducted at the beginning of last year, which naturally had a loss that emerged this year. The second largest factor is the change of collections operations as a result of a change in regulation, which limited the call frequency to consumers.

The next two contributing factors are the industry trend of credit normalization and the negative shock to oil regions in the portfolio.

Once understanding the contributing factors and the sizes of their respective impacts, the lender decided to have further internal discussion to see how to selectively tighten strategies in order to bring the loss level down over the next 12 to 18 months.

16.2.2 Strategy Planning

With a set portfolio risk appetite and a good understanding of the current state, it is time to plan out the strategic actions to be implemented in the next 12 months. Planning is an important exercise every year, so proper resources and time should be allocated to support the business objectives in the coming fiscal period.

One key aspect that will serve to guide the planning is the main objective of portfolio management at the current stage. Different objectives would lead to different prioritizations of various strategies.

For example, one credit card portfolio recently experienced rapid loss growth, which has hindered the portfolio's profitability. Thus, the main objective for the risk team in the following 12 months is to lower the portfolio loss rate.

With the main objective of loss mitigation in mind, the risk team reviewed the available options and planned to focus on the following initiatives:

☑ Review opportunities to scale up or optimize the CLD, high risk closure, and reissue strategies.

☑ Enhance the collections strategies, from delinquent collections to over-limit and pre-delinquency collections. If possible, gain more collections resources or optimize the resource allocation based on risk level and collectability.

☑ Review opportunities to tighten the credit extension strategies such as origination strategy, authorization strategy, and CLI strategies, especially the applications and accounts on the margin.

☑ Also included in the review is whether enough credit is extended to low risk segments. Growing the low risk balance is another way to lower the portfolio loss rate.

In another scenario, a different credit card portfolio has been safely running with the risk level well below the alert level set in its risk appetite statement.

However, the portfolio receivable is staggering, while the competitors are gradually taking market share. The objective for the portfolio in the next 12 months is to regain market share and increase profitability.

Under this circumstance, the risk team focused the planning on the following strategic options:

- ☑ Introduce origination campaigns, via pre-qualified or cross-sell.
- ☑ Review opportunities to expand the authorization and proactive/reactive CLI strategies.
- ☑ Introduce invite-to-apply CLI campaigns.
- ☑ Launch portfolio stimulation campaigns, such as balance transfer and skip-a-payment.

For initiatives that make it to the final plan, high-level timelines and resources need to be mapped out as well. If any gap of resources is identified, it needs to be addressed accordingly.

16.3 Documentation

As many credit decisions might be made over time, especially for revolving credit products such as credit cards, the proper documentation of these decisions is very important to help effectively manage the portfolio over the long term and facilitate possible work transition. It also serves to answer inquiries and audit questions from both the internal audit group and external regulators.

There are several types of documentation that need to be well maintained, which are listed below.

16.3.1 Chronology Log

To facilitate the overall portfolio risk management, it is important to maintain a chronology log of all the changes related to credit policy and strategy.

Senior management and different teams specializing in specific credit decision areas can refer to such a document to quickly grasp the historical changes of the portfolio.

As credit portfolios tend to have risk performance lagging at least 6 to 12 months, this document comes handy to remind people what happened previously, especially when there is a staff turnover.

The format of the chronology log does not need to be fancy. It could be as simple as a list of changes in a spreadsheet or a Word document, with dates of events and brief summaries.

If the impact on risk, balance, and revenue can be quantified and added to the log, that would be even better.

16.3.2 Credit Policy

A copy of the update-to-date credit policy should always be maintained.

Even though I recommend a separation of the credit policy from the often dynamically managed credit strategies, different financial institutions have their own customs regarding the extent of details that the credit policy document should capture.

If a lender chooses to include a great amount of the details of credit strategies in the credit policy document, it needs to make sure that any strategy change is captured there in a timely manner. This could be a challenge if there are multiple strategy changes implemented at the same time, particularly when the policy document includes all lending products.

Sometimes, the credit policy document is maintained at the enterprise level. In this case, an up-to-date copy should be downloaded, or via a link, in a shared folder that the risk team uses for overall documentation purposes.

16.3.3 Strategy Documentation

Credit strategies enable each credit decision throughout the credit life cycle. It is important to maintain a thorough documentation of all the credit strategies, not only for regular day-to-day operations, but also for audit and control purposes.

The following documents are recommended to be kept with an up-to-date version in the centralized risk document repository.

Credit Strategies

Credit strategies are implemented in various credit decision engines. For security purposes, only a small number of people in the financial institution can view the particular rules and settings in each system. Also, it requires special training to understand how to read the strategies directly in the system.

Thus, a copy of each credit strategy should be maintained offline. The document is best organized by each major decision area, and the format needs to be relatively business-user-friendly.

In some cases, the strategy in one decision area consists of disparate logic and settings in various systems. They need to be consolidated in one document to allow a quick overview.

Change-related Documentation

It is also important to maintain good documentation of all credit strategy *changes*. What should be kept in the document repository include:

☑ The presentation material related to a specific strategy change

This usually includes the business case of why a particular change is recommended, estimated impact on P&L, and potential impact on operations. The form could be a PowerPoint deck or a Word document, depending on each financial institution's custom.

☑ The approval of the strategy change

Each strategy change should be approved by someone within the risk organization with the proper authority. The approval itself can be as simple as an email. There are also cases in which a physical signature is required on a sign-off sheet. In that case, the sheet is scanned and a soft copy is saved in the documentation library.

In some financial institutions, besides approval from a first line risk executive, formal approval is also needed from the executives from second line risk and first line business teams. The choice of policy is up to each financial institution.

In reality, even in the case that no formal signature is required from the latter two teams, they will be presented with the proposed changes and their feedback will have been incorporated in the final proposal.

☑ Credit system change request document

Once a credit strategy change is approved, there is often a credit system change request form that needs to be submitted. This is usually required when there is a dedicated credit system team that manages system changes, rather than the credit strategy team itself.

This is an important step, as it is where the business language is translated into technical terms. If not careful, mistakes could happen here. Thus, it is a good practice to keep a record of the specific submitted request.

☑ Testing records

All the testing results should be documented. This includes the testing before the new strategy is released into the production environment. The documentation should record test cases (test scenarios), test accounts, and test results, ideally with relevant screenshots.

After the strategy's release, the production validation result should also be recorded. It could be a sample of an application, transaction, or account, a standard production system report, a custom report, or a description of the production validation activities and results.

16.3.4 Scorecard documentation

For each score used in credit strategies, whether it is a vendor score or is developed internally, the following documentation is recommended to be included in the central depository:

☑ Standard scorecard documentation

This is usually provided when the score is first released.

☑ Ongoing scorecard validation

For vendor scores that are developed for the industry, the vendors would periodically produce their own validation to reflect the latest score odds and key scorecard metrics.

Lenders themselves also monitor the scorecards in use on a regular basis, whether they are developed by vendors or internally. The validation would be just on the lender's own portfolio.

All of these validation reports should be kept in one place.

16.3.5 Manual and Procedure

Every lender also has a manual or procedure document for its operational teams. Such a document usually details step-by-step instructions for performing a specific task.

Since there are many tasks related to credit decisions, such as how to activate a new credit card or how to handle a customer's request to increase the credit line, it would be good for the risk team to keep such a manual or procedure document handy so they can understand the operational aspects as well.

16.4 Strategy Management for Portfolio

This section introduces the recommended rhythm of strategy update and the principle of consistency in strategy management.

16.4.1 Frequency of Strategy Update

How often should a particular strategy be kept in place before you start to develop a new one?

As customer behaviors, portfolio composition, and market conditions are always evolving, you can always find opportunities to fine-tune or redevelop credit strategies.

One approach I would recommend is to always have one challenger strategy alongside the existing champion strategy in each major decision area. This way learning is available to you at all times.

Considering the time needed to have a clear picture of the risk performance, as well as the time required to analyze data and socialize with stakeholders, it could take 12 to 18 months before a conclusion is reached regarding who is the winner between the champion and the challenger strategies.

Of course, in some cases, such as collections strategies, you might be able to reach a conclusion faster — in 6 to 9 months.

On average, it is recommended that you review major credit strategies once a year. What comes out of the review would include a decision on whether the challenger can be claimed as the new champion or not, plus some ideas for the next new challenger strategy to be tested.

Of course, one constraint would be resources available to dedicate to the strategy review and development work, in addition to all other risk management tasks. Business priorities and the availability of adequate support from the credit system team could impact the plan as well.

All of these should be considered when a risk team develops its plan annually.

16.4.2 Strategy Consistency

One thing to pay attention to is that the portfolio risk management should follow a principle of *consistency* in all of its strategies.

Within a Strategy

Consistency should be achieved first within a specific strategy. With a lot of decisions driven by data, it could sometimes happen that the sample data show a result that is counterintuitive. In this case, the data-driven result needs to be overwritten by logical reasoning.

Let's look at the example in Exhibit 16-4, which is part of a collections strategy with collections actions being assigned based on the actual risk performance of each node.

Exhibit 16-4 Strategy Segment with Inconsistent Treatments

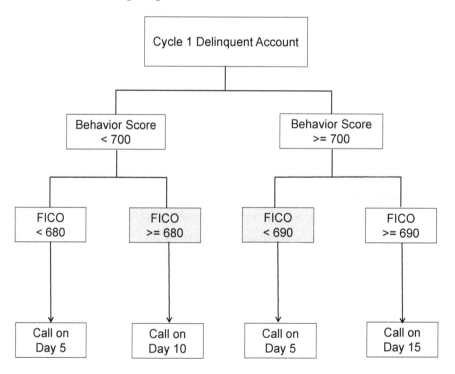

In this exhibit, the population with a behavior score < 700 and FICO between 680 and 689 is assigned a call action on day 10, while the population with a behavior score >= 700 and FICO between 680 and 689 is assigned a call action on day 5.

Within the same FICO range, accounts with higher behavior scores are now assigned with a more aggressive collection action — this is counterintuitive, as higher behavior scores carry lower risk.

In this case, a business decision should be made to override the score cutoffs recommended by data. By changing the FICO cutoff from *680* to *690* for the population with behavior score < 700, the modified strategy, as shown in Exhibit 16-5, eliminates the inconsistency issue.

Exhibit 16-5 Strategy Segment with Consistent Treatments

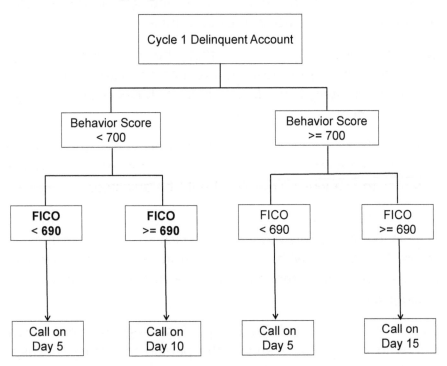

Thus, after the initial strategy has been developed, it is always recommended to go through the entire strategy one more

time to identify and eliminate any inconsistency with common business sense.

Across Different Strategies

Similarly, the consistency principle also applies across different risk strategies.

The reason the inconsistency could happen at the strategy level is that strategies are often managed by different persons or even different teams, which is often the case within a large financial institution. Thus, it is natural that a strategy developer does not know what other strategies are doing to the same accounts.

One example would be that a high risk closure strategy closed a credit card account. Then, the accountholder applied for a new card from the same lender and got approved. This essentially made the account closure futile.

Such a phenomenon reveals that the origination strategy and high risk closure strategy are not consistent. Either the origination strategy is too loose or the high risk closure strategy is too stringent.

When such a case occurs, the persons or teams who manage the origination and high risk closure strategies need to get together to see which strategy should be adjusted.

Ideally, you want to discover the inconsistency before it actually happens. This requires that each strategy developer be somewhat familiar with the credit strategies in other decision areas as well, even though those are not the person's direct responsibilities.

This is where a good inventory of strategy documentation comes in handy. For example, the person managing the high risk closure strategy can take a look at the origination strategy to see what the minimum score cutoff for approval is; and then only close accounts with scores below that cutoff.

Peer review is another way to minimize such inconsistency, i.e., inviting your risk colleagues from other decision areas to take a look at your strategy.

Rotating risk staff across all decision areas is another great way to bring a more holistic view into the strategy development, as the strategy developer already has knowledge of strategies in other areas.

Chapter 17
Portfolio Risk Reports

There are many different portfolio risk reports used by various lenders. This chapter lists some of the most common ones, which would allow you to quickly grasp the latest performance of a credit portfolio and think about potential opportunities to act upon.

Some of these reports would become even more useful if you are able to add relevant benchmark information. Such information usually is available from industry associations, benchmarking companies, credit bureaus, and government agencies.

Even if currently you only work in a specific credit risk decision area, as is often the case in a large bank, it is beneficial to review all the reports available. That would help you establish a holistic portfolio view and better appreciate how your own work fits into the overall picture.

As some of the reports are pretty straightforward and a few others are fairly similar to each other, only selected ones will have the explanations as well as the illustration graphs.

The previous sections have presented some reports specific to each decision area. Here they are not repeated. The focus of this chapter is to present reports typically used for overall portfolio risk management.

17.1 Charge-off and Recovery Reports

As credit loss has a significant impact on a credit portfolio's P&L, loss-related reports are always closely watched by both the risk and the business teams. There are multiple reports to show the loss activities, trends, and different types of losses.

Monthly $ gross charge-off

Every month, the $ gross charge-off is reported. Alongside the same metric from previous months, it is easy to see the $ loss trend over time.

$ gross charge-off rate, 12-month rolling

Because charge-offs lag the origination of the loan balance and the $ charge-off in a given month could come from various origination vintages, the $ charge-off often swings quite a bit from month to month.

To smooth out the fluctuation and better see the trend, a rolling 12-month $ charge-off rate would be a good metric to measure a portfolio's risk level.

The rolling 12-month $ charge-off rate is calculated as:

$ Charge-off in last 12 months / Average balance in last 12 months

Exhibit 17-1 shows a sample graph of the monthly $ gross charge-offs and the rolling 12-month $ charge-off rate.

Exhibit 17-1 Monthly $ CO and Rolling 12-month $ CO Rate

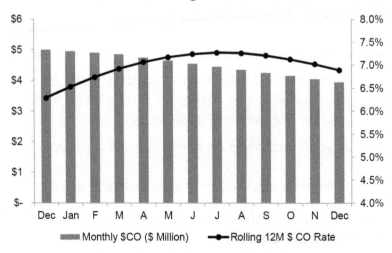

$ gross charge-off rate for the month, annualized

Some people want to focus on the loss experience in the most recent month, so the monthly $ gross charge-off rate can be calculated as:

$ Gross charge-off in the month / Month-end portfolio balance

As the loss rate in risk appetite statement is usually defined as an annual rate, the monthly $ gross charge-off rate multiplied by 12 would be the annualized $ gross charge-off rate for the month.

$ gross charge-off rate for the month, annualized, lagged 6 or 12 months

As loss typically lags the generation of loan balance, it is sometimes not totally fair to calculate the loss rate using the latest month-end balance — especially when there is a large fluctuation of balance, such as a recent large acquisition campaign, or the suddenly shrinking balance, as experienced in early 2020 during the COVID-19 pandemic.

To address this, one can use the balance of 6 months or 12 months earlier, as the loss in the most recent month most likely stems from the balance generated at that time.

The calculation:

Monthly $ gross charge-off / Month-end balance 6 or 12 months ago

charge-off rate, based on active or total accounts

Dollar rate or amount rate is what matters most from a P&L perspective. However, it is also good to see if the # charge-off rate is stable or not, which is defined as:

 # Charge-off accounts in the month / Total # active accounts

Or

 # Charge-off accounts in the month / Total # accounts

The denominator of the latter definition would include both active and inactive accounts.

Reversal rate

For a charge-off account, the balance includes the principal as well as interest and fees accrued on the account. As the principal is the only actual money that a lender loans out, the interest and fees should be reversed from the gross charge-off in order to get the true loss.

The reversal rate is calculated as:

$ Accrued interest and fees on charge-offs / $ Gross charge-offs

Reversal rate and recovery rate are used to convert gross loss into net loss.

Monthly $ recovery

$ recovery in a month measures the dollars collected in this month from accounts already charged off. Please note that this amount is not from the $ gross charge-off that happened in the same month, but rather it is from $ charge-offs in previous months or even years.

Monthly $ recovery rate, portfolio level

At the portfolio level, the $ recovery rate in a given month is calculated as:

$ Recovery in the month / $ Gross charge-off in the month

Even though the $ recovery is not from the $ gross charge-off in the current month, both financial events go into the P&L calculation in the same month. Thus, this metric is used to measure the portfolio-level recovery performance.

If one wants to know how much money can be recouped from a given charge-off vintage, the following report should be used.

Cumulative $ recovery rate, by charge-off vintage

An example of this report has been presented in Chapter 10, Collections, as Exhibit 10-6.

Once having the interest and fees reversed from the gross charge-offs and $ recovery deducted, what is left is the $ net charge-off for which the lender truly loses in the month.

Several reports used to monitor gross charge-offs can be used for net charge-offs as well.

☑ Monthly $ net charge-off

☑ $ net charge-off rate, 12-month rolling

☑ $ net charge-off rate for the month, annualized

☑ $ net charge-off rate for the month, annualized, lagged 6 or 12 months

Bad/Good $ ratio

The bad/good $ ratio is calculated as:

Average $ gross CO balance / Average $ non-CO balance

This metric reflects the lender's capability to control the growth of charge-off balance in relation to the regular account. The lower the ratio, the stronger capability a lender demonstrates in account risk management.

17.2 Charge-off by Category Reports

There are several major types of charge-offs. Credit charge-offs or contractual charge-offs is usually the largest category, which occur due to the deterioration of the borrowers' credit. Other loss types include bankruptcy, deceased, and fraud. As these losses occur for very distinct reasons, they are usually reported separately.

☑ Monthly $ gross charge-off by loss type

☑ Monthly $ percentage of gross charge-off by loss type

Exhibit 17-2 Monthly $ Percentage of Gross Charge-off by Loss Type

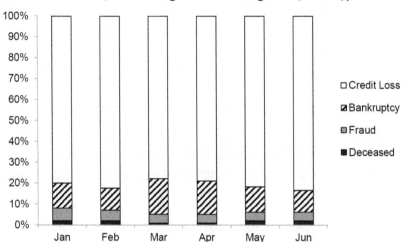

The reports of individual loss types listed below could also have two versions based on gross loss or net loss:

☑ monthly $ credit charge-off

☑ $ credit charge-off rate, 12-month rolling

☑ $ credit charge-off rate of the month, annualized

☑ $ credit charge-off rate of the month, annualized, lagged 6 or 12 months

☑ monthly $ bankruptcy

☑ $ bankruptcy charge-off rate, 12-month rolling

☑ $ bankruptcy charge-off rate of the month, annualized

☑ $ bankruptcy charge-off rate of the month, annualized, lagged 6 or 12 months

☑ # bankruptcy rate, based on active or total accounts

☑ ratio of $ bankruptcy / $ charge-offs

☑ $ credit charge-off recovery rate

☑ $ bankruptcy recovery rate

☑ $ sales proceeds as a percentage of $ recovery (if applicable)

$ net fraud as a percentage of $ net sales

For a revolving product such as credit cards, the fraud activity is typically measured as the ratio of $ net fraud loss against net sales, which consists of both merchandise and cash transactions. The industry average level is usually around 10 bps or 0.1%.

$ net fraud as a percentage of $ net sales, by fraud type

It is important to monitor the composition of the $ fraud loss over time. This helps capture the emerging fraud trend so a lender can tackle the issue before it grows too big and causes more fraud losses.

Typical fraud types include lost and stolen, application fraud, counterfeit, and card not present.

Other typical fraud reports include:

☑ $ net fraud loss amount by fraud type

☑ % of net fraud loss amount by fraud type

☑ monthly $ fraud recovery rate

17.3 Delinquency Reports

17.3.1 Portfolio Delinquency Reports

Delinquency balance precedes the credit loss, thus it is closely watched during portfolio risk monitoring. Typical reports include:

Monthly $ 30+ (60+, 90+) days delinquency

Delinquency is typically reported separately from charge-off.

$ 30+ (60+, 90+) as a percentage of the total portfolio balance

Besides the dollar amount, the $ delinquency as a ratio of the outstanding total is another commonly used metric.

17.3.2 Roll Rate Reports

Roll rate reports are commonly used to reflect the dynamics among different delinquency stages.

Roll rates reflect the effectiveness of collections. Watch for any spike of roll rate in a particular bucket. If this occurs, explore the reasons behind the increase and take corresponding mitigation measures to lower the rate.

Roll rate reports

Roll rate reports are important tools to monitor the effectiveness of collections.

Roll rates can be calculated by # accounts or by $ balance. For the business team, the $ roll rate is more important, as it is closely tied to the portfolio's P&L.

Exhibit 17-3 shows the recent monthly $ roll rates in each different delinquent bucket.

Exhibit 17-3 Monthly $ Roll Rates

Month	Jan	Feb	Mar	Apr	May	Jun
Current to Cycle 1	2.5%	2.4%	2.6%	2.5%	2.5%	2.6%
Cycle 1 to Cycle 2	26.5%	29.0%	27.2%	28.5%	26.9%	27.0%
Cycle 2 to Cycle 3	70.0%	72.0%	71.0%	68.0%	69.0%	71.0%
Cycle 3 to Cycle 4	84.0%	82.0%	85.0%	87.0%	84.0%	86.5%
Cycle 4 to Cycle 5	88.0%	87.7%	87.5%	89.5%	89.1%	87.7%
Cycle 5 to Cycle 6	90.0%	90.5%	91.0%	89.8%	89.5%	90.5%
Cycle 6 to Charge-off	95.0%	95.8%	94.7%	94.0%	96.0%	95.2%

These roll rates are often graphed into line charts, such as Exhibit 17-4 and Exhibit 17-5, so it is easy to spot the trend over time.

Exhibit 17-4 Monthly $ Roll Rates, Cycle 1 to 2 and Cycle 2 to 3

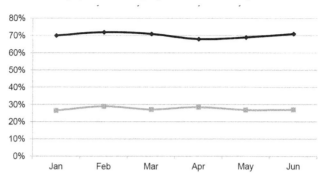

Exhibit 17-5 Monthly $ RollRates, Cycle 3 to 4 and Cycle 4 to 5

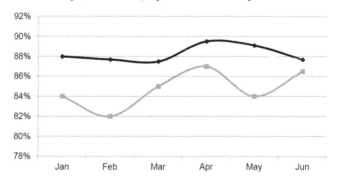

17.3.3 Special Collections Programs

For delinquent accounts, a lender usually has multiple special accommodation programs to help customers go through financial difficulties. These special programs encourage customers to make continuous payments or provide a temporary payment relief, which would help the lender reduce the credit loss as well.

Monthly reports are usually in place to track the # of accounts and their balances under each special program. Such reports include:

Reage report

Lenders usually have a reage policy in place, which allows a delinquent account to be classified as current once the customer makes 3 consecutive monthly minimum payments, even though the total amount of principal, interest, and fee that are contractually due is not 100% collected yet. There are also other qualifying criteria to determine when an account can be reaged.

Reage could be executed by the system or collectors. It is important to monitor the volume of reaged accounts to ensure there is no abuse of this policy, which would make the portfolio quality look better than it actually is.

Forbearance or payment deferral report

Forbearance, also known as payment deferral, allows a customer to skip the payment due for a specified period of time. During the forbearance period, the interest will usually continue to accrue.

As the COVID-19 pandemic started in early 2020, many lenders rolled out forbearance programs for various consumer lending products from mortgages to credit cards. As the result, the report of forbearance programs quickly became one of the most important reports for lenders.

Exhibit 17-6 shows the monthly volume of accounts that enroll and exit the forbearance program and the total number of active enrollments.

Exhibit 17-6 Monthly Volume in Forbearance Plan

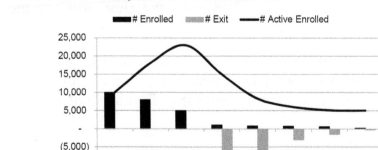

Exhibit 17-7 shows the distribution of account performance after they exit the forbearance program.

These reports are commonly used by lenders to track their forbearance programs during the COVID-19 pandemic.

Exhibit 17-7 Performance of Accounts That Exited from Forbearance

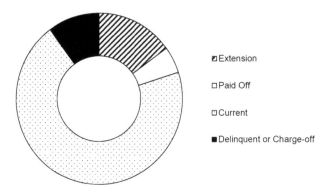

Ø Extension

□ Paid Off

▨ Current

■ Delinquent or Charge-off

Workout report

Some accounts experiencing financial hardship have difficulty keeping up with the original payment schedule. In this case, lenders could provide accountholders with the workout program, under which the customers pay a reduced monthly payment based on a new schedule.

This provides the customers with an alternative to charge-off, which is beneficial to both account holders and lenders. Workout programs can be offered for the short term or the long term, depending on the nature of the hardship.

A typical workout report will track how many accounts have requested the workout plans, how many are approved, the balance in workout programs, and the performance of workout accounts.

Settlement report

As mentioned in Chapter 10, settlement is another alternative option to charge-off.

A settlement report includes the number of settlements each month, the original balance, the settlement amount, and the percentage of the settlement amount over the original balance. The delinquency level, credit bureau score, and collections score at time of settlement can also be part of the report.

17.4 Policy Exception Reports

Another important category of reports are policy exception reports, which include cases that do not conform to the credit policies or strategies.

By having dedicated resources regularly reviewing such exceptions, it helps discover potential issues, whether systematic or caused by human error.

Many exceptions could be legitimate. In this case, the review helps ensure the exceptions are within assigned authority and have proper documentation.

If a breach of approved authority or poor documentation is identified, there is a coaching opportunity for the individuals handling the case. Such a rigorous feedback loop would help reduce the occurrence of similar incidents in the future.

This section lists several types of exception reports just as examples.

17.4.1 Origination Exception Reports

Origination policy exception reports

If we follow the example in Section 5.3 Credit Policy, which lists 5 origination credit policies, the origination policy exception report should capture the following exceptions:

- ☑ Exception of policy 1 — any approved application with a charge-off in the past 24 months.

- ☑ Exception of policy 2 — any approved application with a non-charge-off derogatory record in the past 24 months.

☑ Exception of policy 3 — any approved application if the applicant is not a citizen or permanent immigrant.

☑ Exception of policy 4 — any approved application if the applicant had a previous charge-off with the credit issuer.

☑ Exception of policy 5 — any approved application if the applicant has <=2 trades

Score override reports

Lenders typically have a minimum credit bureau score and a minimum application score requirement in their origination strategies. There should be a report that lists approved applications below the minimum score cut-offs. This is also called a low side override report.

Similarly, there is also a high side override report, which shows the declined applications over the minimum score cut-offs.

There could well be good justifications for these score override decisions. The purpose of the review is to ensure that all exceptions are within assigned authority and well documeted.

Origination limit/loan amount exception reports

Lenders typically have a maximum credit limit assigned at origination. There might even be different maximum credit limits by product or risk segment. Thus, it is beneficial to have an exception report to identify any account with a credit limit assigned over the allowed maximum.

A similar exception report can be developed for installment loans, with the origination limit changed to a loan amount.

17.4.2 Credit Limit Exception Reports

Credit limit management and monitoring is an important part of revolving credit portfolio management. Here are several typical exception reports related to credit limit.

High limit exception report

All revolving credit products have a maximum product limit. The high limit exception report lists all accounts with their credit limit increased beyond the product maximum during a given period.

CLI timing policy exception report

Lenders also have policies regarding the minimum number of month-on-book before a revolving credit account can receive a line increase and the minimum time interval between two line increases.

For example, one credit card issuer only allows the first CLI to be handed out once an account reaches at least 6 month-on-book and the time interval between two CLIs is at least 12 months.

A CLI timing policy exception report would capture any CLI granted before 6 months-of-book and any CLI within 12 months from previous line increase.

17.4.3 Charge-off Exception Reports

Each lender has policies in place to specify when an account should be classified as a particular type of charge-off. Charge-off policy exception reports help ensure that accounts meeting specific charge-off criteria are classified as losses timely, not disguised as good accounts any more.

By charge-off category, the following reports can be established:

- ☑ credit charge-off policy exception
- ☑ bankruptcy charge-off policy exception
- ☑ deceased charge-off policy exception

Such exceptions should be rare, but it is still a good practice to monitor this.

There are also some portfolio activity metrics not directly measuring risk, such as number of accounts, balance, and payments. However, the change of these metrics will impact the risk ratios, so they are often tracked by the risk team as well.

At the end of this book, a list of commonly used reports and their relevant unsecured products is provided in the Appendix for quick reference.

Chapter 18
Manage through Business Cycle

The economy always goes through business cycles. Every business cycle is unique in terms of how long it lasts and what specific event triggered the downturn. However, there are always several main stages in each cycle, at which a credit portfolio can be managed accordingly.

This chapter will introduce how to deploy various tactics to manage an unsecured lending credit portfolio at different stages of a business cycle.
- ☑ Recovery
- ☑ Mid-Cycle
- ☑ Late Cycle
- ☑ Recession

18.1 Recovery

The economy has passed through its worst phase. Business activities begin to pick up, maybe in some sectors before others. The number of job openings starts to grow. The unemployment rate gradually decreases.

Cautious Restart

If you have stopped the major credit expansion initiatives such as prescreen acquisition campaigns or proactive CLI programs, it's now time to restart them, probably with caution.

Some financial institutions might naturally still be concerned about the fragility of the economy during the recovery stage. In this case, you can limit the targets of expansion strategies to just selected segments.

You can always restart with prime and super prime customers. They will bring in high-quality balances to your portfolio, even though there is still risk that some of these customers might not hold their financial footings as the economy is climbing out of the worst days.

Moving down the risk curve, you might also want to target those without prime credit, but they are on the way up. These customers could be young graduates who have just started their careers, or those unemployed during the recession who recently found new jobs.

Credit Momentum Information

Check to see whether your financial institution has already somehow incorporated the credit momentum information in the risk scores. Credit bureaus have various credit attributes to help you assess if a consumer is on an upward or downward credit trajectory.

Look at additional data sources if you are a full-service bank, such as cash flow in and out of the deposit accounts. That will tell you a lot about a consumer's current financial condition.

If your institution does not have the capability to develop scores that can incorporate such momentum information, you can always look at service providers such as FICO and credit bureaus to see if there is any standard off-the-shelf product that you can leverage.

Test Challenger Strategy Early On

It is actually not a bad idea to put in some challenger strategies at this stage, again on a limited portion of the portfolio, to test where you can expand credit further.

Given the typical amount of time it takes to read the performance of a new risk strategy, it is recommended that you test the challenger early on during the business cycle. This way, you can read the result and act soon enough to reap the opportunity once the economy is back in a solid growth mode in mid-cycle.

Overall, you do not want to stay in the full defense mode that was adopted for the recession period for too long. You need to stay in the market. Continue to open for business, although cautiously.

Lending is a business of risk and reward. You have to take some calculated risk in order to gain business. A good time to do so would be in the recovery phase.

When you get prepared with all the supplies and head out to climb a mountain, you need to start early. Maybe it is still dark outside, but you know the sun will rise soon. By heading out early, you give yourself plenty of time to ascend. You can also go a bit faster when there is less traffic.

18.2 Mid-Cycle

The Growth Period

After recovering from the bottom of the recession, the economy continues to expand. The number of job openings keeps growing. The unemployment rate gradually trends toward the long-term average level. Business activities become even more active.

This is the period in which your credit portfolio can experience decent growth, along with the economy and the credit market.

Since you have laid the groundwork in the recovery phase by resuming and testing some expansion strategies, you would have some readings to know which parts of the strategies are working and which parts need further adjustments.

By analyzing customer behaviors and credit performance, you also know which customer segments are the best ones to engage further.

Equipped with the actual performance from early tests, you can confidently roll out the expansion strategies to a larger scale, if you have not done that already.

With the new champion strategies in place, you can even begin the next round of challenger strategies in order to test new segments and new treatments.

Ride the Growth Wave

Your overall risk strategy shifts more from pure loss mitigation toward supporting business growth during the best time. With the collaboration with the business team and other stakeholder groups, your portfolio is positioned well to ride the growth phase of the current cycle.

If you have stayed ahead of your competition with prudent expansions, you should be able to grow your portfolio and even gain some market share, without sacrificing credit quality.

It is also a time to evaluate any opportunity to make strategic investments, whether on technical tools or analytical resources, in order to expand your risk analytics capability.

During your mountain climbing journey, your vision gets much better when the sun comes out. This is the period where you could make great strides. As you ascend further, you assess the environment and choose the best path forward. You might have to make new trails, as nobody has set foot in this territory yet.

18.3 Late Cycle

The economy has now been steadily growing for almost a decade. The unemployment rate is approaching historical lows. Businesses begin to have difficulty hiring qualified people.

There are job postings everywhere, from coffee shops to grocery stores to restaurants.

Stocks are up. The real estate market is hot and competing offers abound. Everything seems to defy the law of gravity.

Reduce Unwanted Exposure

This is the time to quietly brush the dust off your exposure reduction strategies, if they have not been deployed with scale for a while. Via CLD and inactive closure, you want to remove some unwanted exposure before the economy tide shifts.

Some lenders begin to review their business lines and might make some strategic exit decisions. At the same time, other companies are still rolling out new products. There is nothing wrong with the new product release, but you need to be prepared to hit the brakes at any time.

Get Prepared

It helps to begin thinking about the recession scenario, something maybe nobody likes to talk about except the risk folks. Don't be afraid to be the pessimist in the room at this moment. You don't want to stop the business, just inject some caution into discussions and decisions.

If you are using historical data to review a strategy, always add in some additional cushion to cover the possibility of an upcoming recession. The farther you are from last recession, the more likely you'll run into a new one in the next few years.

In this phase, you are approaching the peak of the mountain, enjoying the thrill and the beautiful view near the top. However, getting to the top is only half the job. What is more important, and many people do not realize this, is that you need to descend safely.

In order to achieve that, you need to have a good idea about the time and resources that you need to come down with safety.

Descending needs time, so you do not want to do it too late. Start to descend when the sun is still out there and the condition has not deteriorated yet. Also, make sure you have the right supplies and tools.

18.4 Recession

During a recession, business activities stall and the economy contracts. The unemployment rate shoots back up. Consumers and businesses have difficulties keeping up with payments. Delinquencies and defaults are on the rise.

When a recession hits, lenders quickly enter a recession management mode.

Review and Documentation

For more prepared lenders, a playbook of recession management might have been discussed during a recent cycle. However, it is still important to review all available options to manage the loss down, as every recession is different and new plays will probably be needed.

You might not need to make all the plays at once, but it is important to go through them and have a good discussion. Document the decision and reasons for it — the decision also includes *No Action* in a particular decision area — the documentation will be useful for future portfolio management, internal audit, and regulatory review.

Strategy Tightening

Lenders usually want to tighten the credit strategies in order to mitigate potential losses in the upcoming recession.

Depending on the specific recession scenario, a lender's particular business model, and its customer base, the degrees of tightening often vary among different lenders.

Generally, all proactive credit extension initiatives will be significantly scaled back, such as prescreen or proactive CLI. Regular acquisition and authorization strategies will be subject to review and will tighten accordingly.

CLD and closure activities will be reinforced. Collections operations will be busy with the high volume. Special collection programs such as hardship and settlement will be utilized more often.

Frequent Reporting

Ideally, you've already done enough work to make all the reports covered in previous chapters readily available. This would serve as a good foundation to stay on top of your portfolio dynamics. Now is a time to focus attention on the more important ones.

An example would be how much your new origination is from below prime vs. prime and the super prime population. Investors and regulators have a keen interest in knowing this.

Another example would be the exposure reduction report, which can show how your strategies are proactively reducing the high risk exposure.

As a recession sets in and is prolonged, the old historical data is less likely to provide an accurate prediction of the future. A natural response would be to increase the frequency of reporting, so stakeholders can access the latest information quickly. Monthly reports become weekly or even daily reports. Leveraging technology and having automated reports will be a great help.

Product Sustainability

On the business side, this is the time product sustainability gets the ultimate test. Products that did not generate much profit even during the good times could easily become money losers in a deteriorating environment. Some products would not be able to survive the recession.

Most fatalities during mountain climbing actually happen on the way down from the peak. If you were prepared in advance, you will have avoided descending in the dark, blanketed by a blizzard, along with a lot of fellow people on a narrow path that is clearly prone to tragedy.

You want to safely descend to the base and restore your energy. There is always the next mountain waiting for you to climb.

As a summary, Exhibit 18-1 provides a brief guidance of available strategy options in each phase of a business cycle.

18.5 Trends to Watch in the Next Cycle

In the second half of 2020, as this book was written, the whole world was still wrestling with the rampant COVID-19 pandemic. Some of the trends such as online purchase and telehealth had already started before the pandemic, but COVID-19 definitely accelerated the advancement of these trends.

Similarly, for risk management, there are a few trends that potentially will be bolstered and generate significant impacts in the next decade. The practice of risk management will continue to evolve as we go through the pandemic and enter the next business cycle.

Automation

Today, there is still a lot of repetitive manual work in retail risk management or consumer lending in general, where efficiency is paramount in order to build up scale and manage cost down. Automation of those repetitive tasks will free up precious human capital, which can be better used for important discussion and decision making. A high degree of automation will help businesses move forward rapidly.

Explainable AI

Artificial Intelligence (AI) has gained some traction in the banking industry in recent years. The chatbot has been used

Exhibit 18-1 Strategy Options During Business Cycles

Recovery	Mid-Cycle	Late Cycle	Recession
• Gradually restart or scale up a prescreen campaign (via score cut-off, etc.). • Restart or scale up a balance transfer campaign (via score cut-off, MOB, etc.). • Restart or scale up CLI (via score cut-off, CLI interval, MOB, etc.). • Launch new challenger strategies in origination, authorization, CLI, etc. by easing up on selected segments.	• Aim to optimize the credit strategies of origination, authorization, CLI, balance transfer, etc. in the current economic environment. • Claim new champion strategies based on earlier tests in order to embrace the growth opportunities fully. • Launch new challenger strategies to further test new segments and new treatments.	• Review and beef up CLD, high risk closure, and inactive closure strategies in order to remove high risk and unused exposure. • Increase the buffer in the loss estimate during risk strategy development. • Review systems and processes; make necessary investment in resources to support fast risk mitigation actions whenever needed.	• Stop or scale back the prescreen campaign (via score cut-off, etc.); increase income verification. • Stop or scale back the balance transfer campaign (via score cut-off, MOB, etc.). • Stop or scale back CLI (via score cut-off, CLI interval, MOB, etc.). • Tighten origination strategy where it makes sense (via score cut-off, key credit attributes, limit assigned, etc.) • Tighten authorization strategy where it makes sense (via score cut-off, MOB, days delinquency allowed, overlimit cushion, etc.) • Beef up CLD, high risk closure, and inactive closure strategies. • Beef up pre-delinquency, overlimit, and delinquency collection strategies; increase the usage of forbearance, workout, settlement, and legal programs where they fit; consider bad debt sales or outsourcing where it makes sense.

in customer service successfully to take care of some basic inquiries.

AI is a promising technology for enhancing risk monitoring, detection, and response. AML and fraud are a couple of areas that show the impact first. However, it is important for users to understand how the output from the AI model is derived. Being a black box does not help adoption. Thus explainable AI comes in nicely to leverage AI technology, but at the same time is able to make the decision process more transparent. Looking forward to seeing this gets applied more in risk strategy design, which currently still takes time.

New Financial Services Ecosystem

Fintech companies once were presented as the disruptors of the incumbent financial institutions. Over time, some of them have been absorbed into the overall financial ecosystem via partnership with incumbents or direct acquisition. It would be interesting to see how the industry continues to evolve and leverage the technology solutions pioneered by fintechs, big techs, and leading incumbent institutions.

Cloud

Cloud-based infrastructure and services will continue to overtake the financial industry. The early adopter Capital One closed its last data center and became a cloud-enabled bank in 2020[1]. In the same year, IBM announced its intention to divest itself from its traditional infrastructure services segment and focus on hybrid-cloud solutions[2].

In the coming years, more lenders will begin to move their data into the cloud environment — on-premises or off-premises. As a result, cloud-based risk management and analytical solutions will also plug in nicely.

Distributed Workforce

With the pandemic, the traditional workforce arrangement is expected to transition into a mixed model with working remotely in combination with group collaboration in the office. The more distributed workforce model would allow companies to source talents from a bigger pool across multiple geographical locations. This will probably lead to more competition for the best risk talent.

Stay Connected

I hope this book has helped you gain a good understanding of the overall risk management practices for unsecured lending portfolios.

Although your reading journey has come to an end, I welcome you to stay connected in one of the following ways.

Write a Book Review

Did the book meet your expectations? Are there any specific things you like about the book and/or anything it can do better? Please kindly leave a review of the book online.

Readers' reviews are very important for an author. Your honest feedback will help others see the true value of this book. I will personally read every review that is posted. It will also help me make enhancements to the book's future editions. I thank you for this in advance.

Share Your Experience

If you have a chance to apply what you have learned from this book, whether it is strategy development, scorecard monitoring, or portfolio management, I would love to hear your experience. Does any content of this book help your specific project? Is there anything else you wish you could know before diving into your work? I would welcome your feedback.

Ask Questions

To make the content of the book easy to consume, the length of the book has intentionally been kept under 300 pages. As a result, some topics are not covered in this book, while those included might not be sufficiently in depth for some readers.

If you have any questions, you can reach out and I shall do my best to answer them.

Share Your Thoughts

Due to possible limitations or gaps in my experience, there is a good chance that you have different and better thoughts regarding the philosophy, framework, methodology, or practices in unsecured lending risk management. I would like to hear your thoughts. We can all learn from each other and advance the practice of retail risk management, which is always evolving.

Thank you for purchasing and reading the book. I certainly hope it will help you launch or advance your career in unsecured lending risk management!

Best regards,

Frank

Email: gangxing_tian@hotmail.com

Appendix:
Frequently Used Reports

Report Name	Credit Card	Line of Credit	Installment Loan	Overdraft
Charge-off & Recovery Reports				
Monthly $ gross charge-off	x	x	x	x
$ gross charge-off rate, 12-month rolling	x	x	x	x
$ gross charge-off rate for the month, annualized	x	x	x	x
$ gross charge-off rate for the month, annualized, lagged 6 or 12 months	x	x	x	x
# charge-off rate, based on active accounts	x	x		x
# charge-off rate, based on total accounts	x	x	x	x
Reversal rate	x	x	x	x
Monthly $ recovery	x	x	x	x
Monthly $ recovery rate, portfolio level	x	x	x	x
Cumulative $ recovery rate, by charge-off vintage	x	x	x	x
Monthly $ net charge-off	x	x	x	x
$ net charge-off rate, 12-month rolling	x	x	x	x
$ net charge-off rate for the month, annualized	x	x	x	x
$ net charge-off rate for the month, annualized, lagged 6 or 12 months	x	x	x	x
Bad/Good $ ratio	x	x	x	x
Charge-off by Category Reports				
Monthly $ gross charge-off by loss type	x	x	x	x
Monthly $ percentage of gross charge-off by loss type	x	x	x	x
Monthly $ credit charge-off	x	x	x	x
$ credit charge-off rate, 12-month rolling	x	x	x	x
$ credit charge-off rate of the month, annualized	x	x	x	x
$ credit charge-off rate of the month, annualized, lagged 6 or 12 months	x	x	x	x
Monthly $ bankruptcy	x	x	x	x
$ bankruptcy charge-off rate, 12-month rolling	x	x	x	x
$ bankruptcy charge-off rate of the month, annualized	x	x	x	x
$ bankruptcy charge-off rate of the month, annualized, lagged 6 or 12 months	x	x	x	x
# bankruptcy rate, based on active accounts	x	x		x
# bankruptcy rate, based on total accounts	x	x	x	x
Ratio of $ bankruptcy / $ charge-offs	x	x	x	x
$ credit charge-off recovery rate	x	x	x	x
$ bankruptcy recovery rate	x	x	x	x
$ sales proceeds as a percentage of $ recovery	x	x	x	x
$ net fraud as a percentage of $ net sales	x	x		x
$ net fraud as a percentage of $ net sales, by fraud type	x	x		x
$ net fraud loss amount by fraud type	x	x	x	x
% net fraud loss amount by fraud type	x	x	x	x
Monthly $ fraud recovery rate	x	x	x	x

Report Name	Credit Card	Line of Credit	Installment Loan	Overdraft
Delinquency Reports				
Monthly $ 30+ (60+, 90+) days delinquency	x	x	x	x
$ 30+ (60+, 90+) as a percentage of the total portfolio balance	x	x	x	x
Roll rate reports, # rate	x	x	x	x
Roll rate reports, $ rate	x	x	x	x
Reage report	x	x	x	x
Forbearance or payment deferral report	x	x	x	x
Workout report	x	x	x	x
Settlement report	x	x	x	x
Policy Exception Reports				
Origination Exception Reports				
Origination policy exception reports	x	x	x	x
Score override reports	x	x	x	x
Origination limit/loan amount exception reports	x	x	x	x
Credit Limit Exception Reports				
High limit exception report	x	x		x
CLI timing policy exception report	x	x		x
Charge-off Exception Reports				
Credit charge-off policy exception report	x	x	x	x
Bankruptcy charge-off policy exception report	x	x	x	x
Deceased charge-off policy exception report	x	x	x	x
Portfolio Activity Reports				
Total portfolio balance and annual growth rate	x	x	x	x
Total # accounts and annual growth rate	x	x	x	x
Percentage of $ payment out of the total balance	x	x	x	x
Total revolving balance and annual growth rate	x			
Total # active accounts and annual growth rate	x	x		x
Total # revolving accounts and annual growth rate	x			
# active accounts as a percentage of total accounts	x	x		x
Percentage of balance revolving	x			
Percentage of accounts revolving	x			
Percentage of active accounts, revolving only	x			
Percentage of active accounts, transactor/convenience only	x			
Average balance of active accounts and annual growth rate	x	x		x
Average balance of active accounts, revolving only	x			
Average balance of active accounts, transactor/convenience only	x			
Average utilization of total accounts (active accouts, current accounts)	x	x		x
Involuntary attrition as a percentage of total accounts	x	x		x
Sales Reports				
Net sales per active account	x	x		x
Net cash advance per active account	x	x		x
Net sales and cash advance per active account	x	x		x
# net sales transactions per active account	x	x		x
# net cash advance transactions per active account	x	x		x
# net total transactions per active account	x	x		x
$ average amount per sales transaction	x	x		x
$ average amount per cash transaction	x	x		x

Endnote

Chapter 2

1. U.S. Bureau of Economic Analysis. Shares of gross domestic product: Personal consumption expenditures [DPCERE1Q156NBEA]. Retrieved on November 23, 2020 from FRED, Federal Reserve Bank of St. Louis; https://fred.stlouisfed.org/series/DPCERE1Q156NBEA.

2. Federal Reserve Bank of New York. November 2020. Quarterly Report on Household Debt and Credit.

3. Board of Governors of the Federal Reserve System. November 2020. Report to the Congress on the Profitability of Credit Card Operations of Depository Institutions.

4. Ibid.

5. The Institute of Internal Auditors. 2013. The Three Lines of Defense in Effective Risk Management and Control, adapted from ECIIA/ FERMA Guidance on the 8th EU Company Law Directive, article 41.

Chapter 3

1. VantageScore is developed by the three national credit reporting companies (Equifax, Experian and TransUnion). For details, please see https://vantagescore.com.

2. Siddiqi, Naeem. 2006. Credit Risk Scorecards: Developing and Implementing Intelligent Credit Scoring. Hoboken, New Jersey: John Wiley & Sons, Inc. Pp. 166-167.

Chapter 4

1. Equifax claims to have personally identifiable information to over 222 million U.S. consumers. Retrieved on January 23, 2021 from https://www.equifax.com/business/consumer-credit-file/.

Chapter 5

1. A score vendor might choose to rank its scores differently. For example, Experian's Bankruptcy PLUS score uses high value to

indicate high risk. Retrieved on February 3, 2021 from https://www.experian.com/assets/consumer-information/product-sheets/bankruptcy-plus.pdf.

2. Consumer Financial Protection Bureau. 12 CFR Part 1026.51 Ability to Pay. Retrieved on January 23, 2021 from https://www.consumerfinance.gov/rules-policy/regulations/1026/51/#a-2-ii-B.

3. Consumer Financial Protection Bureau. 12 CFR Part 1002.9 Notifications. Retrieved on January 23, 2021 from https://www.consumerfinance.gov/rules-policy/regulations/1002/9/.

Chapter 7

1. FICO and Fiserv. May 2020. Client Webinar Series: Credit Risk Exposure Management — Credit Line & Authorization Strategy.

Chapter 8

1. Consumer Financial Protection Bureau. August 2019. The Consumer Credit Card Market. Pp. 95-96.

2. Consumer Financial Protection Bureau. 12 CFR Part 1026.51 Ability to Pay. Retrieved on January 23, 2021 from https://www.consumerfinance.gov/rules-policy/regulations/1026/51/#a-2-ii-B.

3. Government of Canada. September 2009. Credit Business Practices Regulations (SOR/2009-257). Retrieved on January 23, 2021 from https://laws-lois.justice.gc.ca/eng/regulations/SOR-2009-257/page-1.html.

Chapter 10

1. Federal Communications Commission. FCC Actions on Robocalls, Telemarketing. Retrieved on February 3, 2021 from: https://www.fcc.gov/general/telemarketing-and-robocalls#:~:text=In%20an%20effort%20to%20address,artificial%20or%20prerecorded%20voice%20messages..

2. Consumer Financial Protection Bureau. 12 CFR Part 1006 Debt Collection Practices (Regulation F). Retrieved on January 24, 2021 from https://files.consumerfinance.gov/f/documents/cfpb_debt-collection_final-rule_2020-10.pdf.

Chapter 12

1. Examples include Citi Flex Loan, American Express Plan It, and CIBC Pace It installment loans. Information retrieved on February 3, 2021 from the company websites.

2. American Bankers Association. The Industry Responds to the Coronavirus. Retrieved on February 3, 2021 from https://www. aba.com/about-us/press-room/industry-response-coronavirus.

3. Canadian Bankers Association. January 26, 2021. Focus: Fast facts on bank measures in response to the COVID-19 pandemic. Retrieved on February 3, 2021 from https://cba.ca/fast-facts-on-bank-measures-in-response-to-the-covid-19-pandemic.

Chapter 18

1. Roberto Torres. November 19, 2020. 'Do the hard things first': What Capital One prioritized in its cloud migration. Retrieved on February 3, 2021 from: https://www.bankingdive.com/news/capital-one-cloud-migration-journey-allison-perkel/589355/.

2. IBM. October 8, 2020. IBM To Accelerate Hybrid Cloud Growth Strategy And Execute Spin-Off Of Market-Leading Managed Infrastructure Services Unit. Retrieved on February 3, 2021 from https://newsroom.ibm.com/2020-10-08-IBM-To-Accelerate-Hybrid-Cloud-Growth-Strategy-And-Execute-Spin-Off-Of-Market-Leading-Managed-Infrastructure-Services-Unit.

Index

Ingram Content Group UK Ltd.
Milton Keynes UK
UKHW021301240423
420691UK00022B/685